WRITERS AN[...]

Chief Editor

A. NORMAN JEFFARES

Advisory Editors

DAVID DAICHES   C. P. SNOW

JAMES JOYCE is recognised as a major figure in the literary scene of the first quarter of the twentieth century, and was probably the most important experimental novelist of the period. His effort to portray the whole meaning of modern life—its fragmentation, its hidden recesses, its underlying patterns—led to a life-long search for ways of doing so. Realism, myth, symbolism, the "stream of consciousness," multiple planes of reality, all became part of an artistic process that finally involved the disruption and recreation of language itself.

In this study, S. L. Goldberg traces the development of Joyce's work from the early sketches and poems, through his masterpiece, *Ulysses*, to the ambitious failure of the all-embracing "history of the world," *Finnegans Wake*. Joyce's preoccupation with the nature of art and the artist's place in society, with the understanding of life and the "joy" he tried to express in his own art, are traced with judgment and discernment. There is an illuminating commentary on Joyce's techniques and on the main lines of Joycian criticism.

S. L. Goldberg read English at the Universities of Melbourne and Oxford. After obtaining a B. Litt. at Oxford, he returned to teach at Melbourne, and at Sydney, where he was Professor of English Literature. He is now Robert Wallace Professor of English in the University of Melbourne and editor of *The Critical Review: Melbourne-Sydney*. His publications include *The Classical Temper* (1961), a study of Joyce, and critical essays on a variety of subjects.

JOYCE

S. L. GOLDBERG

OLIVER AND BOYD

EDINBURGH AND LONDON

OLIVER AND BOYD LTD
Tweeddale Court
Edinburgh 1

39A Welbeck Street
London W. 1

First published 1962
Reprinted 1965
Reprinted 1967

Printed in Great Britain for Oliver and Boyd Ltd
by Robert MacLehose and Co. Ltd, Glasgow

CONTENTS

ACKNOWLEDGMENTS

Thanks are due to the Society of Authors, as the literary representative of the Estate of the late James Joyce, for permission to reproduce all quotations from his works, in particular those from *The Critical Writings of James Joyce*, *Finnegans Wake*, and *Letters of James Joyce*.

Acknowledgments are due to the following publishers in respect of quotations from the works of James Joyce indicated: The Bodley Head and Random House Inc. (*Ulysses*); Jonathan Cape Ltd and Viking Press Inc. (*Dubliners*, *Exiles*, *A Portrait of the Artist as a Young Man*); Jonathan Cape Ltd and New Directions (*Stephen Hero*); Faber and Faber Ltd and Viking Press Inc. (*The Critical Writings of James Joyce*, *Finnegans Wake*, *Letters of James Joyce*).

Acknowledgment is also due to Oxford University Press Inc., New York, for permission to reproduce quotations from Richard Ellmann, *James Joyce*.

The photograph on the front cover is reproduced by permission of Dr G. Freund.

S.L.G.

ABBREVIATED TITLES
BY WHICH JOYCE'S WORKS AND SOME OTHERS
ARE CITED IN THE TEXT

JOYCE'S WORKS

Where two page numbers are given, the first refers to the current English edition, the second (in brackets) to the American. For full details, see the Bibliography.

C.M.	=	*Chamber Music*, ed. William York Tindall.
C.W.	=	*The Critical Writings of James Joyce*.
D.	=	*Dubliners*.
F.W.	=	*Finnegans Wake*: all cloth edns have the same pagination.
L.	=	*Letters of James Joyce*.
P.	=	*A Portrait of the Artist as a Young Man*. References to London 1956 followed by New York 1928 etc.
S.H.	=	*Stephen Hero*. References to rev. edn., London 1956 followed by New York 1955.
U.	=	*Ulysses*. References to London 1937, etc., followed by London 1960; followed by New York 1940 etc.

OTHERS

E.	=	Richard Ellmann, *James Joyce*.
J.J.M.	=	*A James Joyce Miscellany*, ed. Marvin Magalaner.
J.J.M.S.	=	*A James Joyce Miscellany*, Second Series, ed. Marvin Magalaner.
J.J.R.	=	*The James Joyce Review*.
M.B.K.	=	Stanislaus Joyce, *My Brother's Keeper*.
T.D.C.	=	*James Joyce: Two Decades of Criticism*, ed. Seon Givens.

CHAPTER I

THE DEVELOPMENT OF THE ARTIST

When Joyce started writing, his intention was both pure and simple: to express his own feelings honestly and to tell the truth about the world he knew. Hardly had he started, however, when he realised that his feelings were part of that world—and then that his world was part of him. To tell the whole truth, he had to portray himself truthfully as well. This he was willing enough to do, of course; after all, what subject could he be more interested in or more truthful about? But now the truth was rapidly appearing less pure and less simple—for how could he distinguish, in what was formed by his imagination, between what he *saw* and what he *felt*, and yet unless he did so, how could he discern what was of objective, and therefore of universal, significance in his experience? To see this difficulty was the first step to understanding a good deal more both about himself and about other people. Thus he came at last to realise that the central thing he had to tell the truth about was his own attempt to tell the truth, to search for the meaning of his own experience. The subject of his art became the nature of art and its tangled relations with life, personal and social. And with this step he moved out of the comparatively clear-cut world of nineteenth-century fiction into the bewildering, multiple, self-reflexive "realities" of the twentieth century. His early sketches and poems had brought the young man to *Dubliners* and *Stephen Hero*, these in turn to *A Portrait of the Artist as a Young Man*, and thence to his masterpiece, *Ulysses*; after that, there remained the all-embracing ambitiousness of *Finnegans Wake*, "a history of the world."[1]

This, broadly, is the literary "case" Joyce represents, and it explains why his career has provided not one, but two attractive myths: the characteristically nineteenth-century myth of the great artist who struggled against conventional morality in order to tell the truth about his society, and the characteristically twentieth-century myth of the great *avant-garde* experimentalist who struggled to break with all accepted values and forms, even with language itself, in order to produce a literary revolution. That Joyce himself was partly responsible for these myths did not prevent him from also becoming partly their victim; but if we turn from his "autobiographical" writings to his actual career (which a group of devoted scholars have recently opened to our view), and realise that his artistic "self-image," Stephen Dedalus, is less a personal vindication than a hard-won imaginative creation, we begin to see that such myths are misleading not only about his greatness but even about his struggles.

Three of Joyce's literary heroes were Ibsen, Blake, and Dante, and like theirs, his most difficult battles were "spiritual," within himself, though his time and place largely set the terms in which those battles were to be fought.[2] He was born in Dublin on 2 February 1882, the eldest son of a large middle-class family whose fortunes were soon rapidly to decline—an environment whose influence he never escaped. The external circumstances of his life between 1882 and 1898 (when he left school) are more or less accurately reflected in his early works: the wanderings about Dublin in boyhood; the general economic stagnation and political bitterness he observed, even in his home; his father's alcoholic fecklessness and the poverty and strain it produced; his own scholastic success at Clongowes Wood College and later at Belvedere College under his Jesuit masters; his early religiosity; the sexual turbulence of his adolescence; the limited but pleasant social life he enjoyed as a youth in Dublin; then his break from religion and from the conventional, rather tarnished, ideals his masters and family seemed to set before him; his matriculation to University College, Dublin, in 1898; and his now articulate desire to be an "artist." What his early works do not portray, however, is the aspect of his character that earned him the family nickname, "Sunny Jim"—his responsiveness, his humour, his quick gaiety, the qualities that made him (unlike Stephen Dedalus) both popular with others and capable of deep personal affection. Perhaps it was this very capacity for affection that caused the first of his struggles with himself and encouraged a certain enigmatic quality in his personality. We can only speculate how far the quarrels between his parents split his affections and forced on him a self-protective detachment; he obviously regretted any estrangement from either, and everything he did and wrote testifies to his abiding family-love. But certainly he was bitterly hurt by the split between his own profound moral and religious sense and the visible manifestations of Irish Catholicism, just as he was hurt later on by the split between his love for Ireland, which led him to desire nothing more than to change her completely for the better, and the disdain with which she seemed to reward his loving denunciations. These were frustrations that evoked the tactic of "silence, exile and cunning" which he bestowed on the young Stephen Dedalus,[3] though he himself could never quite fully adopt it however hard he tried. Yet the capacity for proud, cold, aloof, egotistic, almost ruthless self-determination was present in him from the first; it was the other side of "Sunny Jim" that at once baffled and attracted the serviceable hero-worship of his younger brother, Stanislaus, as it was to do with many others in later life.[4]

What he carried over from this period of his life is revealed by the *Portrait*. Since Ireland at the time could offer little more than the conventional values he had soon begun to question, he was bound to fall back on the only resource he had—his still highly immature self. What was more, the narrow traditions of life and art available to him there meant that any partial rejection was bound to grow wider, that any friendship was bound to be tested to the limit, and that any career he wished to commit himself to fully, mind and body, heart and soul, was bound to appear to him as a quasi-religious vocation, a deliberate alternative to, but yet a form of, priesthood.[5] Again, the religion he had eagerly embraced and then rejected inevitably left its mark, as he realised himself. His attraction to ritual and theology was only one result; there were also the superstitious fears that continually nagged him. There was the never quite fully acknowledged self-consciousness about sex, which reinforced what his brother thought was the Irishman's natural tendency to regard women as biological functions.[6] There were the wide knowledge, the highly-developed memory, and the businesslike shrewdness his Jesuit schooling had given him. There was, too, the deep, ineradicable love of rules, extrinsic order, encyclopaedic system, which led him to read Aquinas for himself and admire him as "perhaps the keenest and most lucid mind known to human history"[7] —a tendency that was, like these others, to be at once a source of strength and weakness.[8] And there was the sense he partly imbibed from his teachers that the truest sort of heroism lay in moral courage—the impulse that led him even as a schoolboy to choose Ulysses as his "favourite hero."[9] But his interests in literature in this period reveal exactly the kind of eager, unsophisticated idealism we should expect: the Romantic poets, especially Shelley, Byron, and Blake; then the Victorian novelists; and finally, and above all, Ibsen. What we know of his own juvenilia reveals the spirit in which he read them: an abortive book of poems called (with a significant vagueness) "Moods," and an abortive book of sketches, uncertainly naturalistic in approach, called (again significantly) "Silhouettes."[10]

The second major period of his life is that between 1898, when he entered University College, and 1904, when at last he shook the dust of Ireland off his feet. This is the period in which he grew, with remarkable speed, into self-conscious articulateness, in which he assumed charge of his mind and of his life. His reading was now wider, including a host of authors who influenced his mind and taste: Giordano Bruno, Dante, D'Annunzio, Flaubert; George Moore, Yeats, Arthur Symons on *The Symbolist Movement*, and some of the Symbolists themselves; Aristotle, Aquinas, Shakespeare, Jonson—to name but a few. He formed the friendships that were to be reflected in the *Portrait* and *Ulysses*; he became acquainted with George Russell (and his Theosophical interests), Yeats, and other leading spirits of the Irish Revival; but he also found himself held apart from others by his uncompromising stand for European rather than native tendencies in literature, and by his firm (and rather prickly) conviction that his own direction lay elsewhere. However, at this stage we can begin to follow his convictions as he formulated them himself.

There is, however, one popular fallacy to get rid of at the start. Many readers, taking the *Portrait* too literally as autobiography, have assumed that in his artistic outlook Joyce sprang fully armed at the age of eighteen or so from the head of St Thomas Aquinas. Nothing could be further from the truth. If his ideas sprang from anywhere, it was from the Romantics, and particularly from Shelley; but, in fact, once he began thinking about art, his attitudes developed as he developed himself. Where his novels do help us is in their continual insistence that the way his attitudes evolved, the process of his maturation, is the Ariadne's thread to the Dedalan maze. And as we examine his attitudes to his "vocation" we cannot but agree. What really matters is not any comprehensive theory about art that we can construct from his writings, but rather the slow, uneven, not always obvious deepening of his insight: which means, in practice, that very often we need to understand the limitations of his understanding at a particular time even more, perhaps, than the immediate point he was concerned to make.

This applies especially to his early manifestoes. The first was a paper delivered to his College Literary and Historical Society in 1900, "Drama and Life."[11] Its immediate purpose was to defend his hero, Ibsen: his plays "let in fresh air," their unconventionality was really the sign of artistic truth and freedom, above all they manifested the genuine "spirit" of drama. The rhetoric is at once self-conscious, eager, and dogmatic, and the Shelleyan echoes are unmistakable. The essay even suffers from the same basic confusions as Shelley's *Defence of Poetry*: "drama" is confounded with art as a whole, and it is conceived as some vaguely transcendental "spirit" of human life itself. But Joyce's central propositions all reveal a kind of "Platonism," an attitude he was later to reject (or at least to qualify) in *Ulysses* and, later still, to surrender to completely in *Finnegans Wake*. Thus "human society is the embodiment of changeless laws" underlying the "accidental manners and humours" of a particular society; "drama," or art proper, has to do with the first, while the second is the concern of mere "literature"; and by "drama," he continues,

I understand the interplay of passions to portray truth; drama is strife, evolution, movement in whatever way unfolded; it exists, before it takes form, independently; it is conditioned but not controlled by its scene.[12]

Nevertheless, he does grasp certain insights quite firmly. The only proper source and subject and justification of art lies in the moral life of human beings "as we see it before our eyes"; and, since its only essential function is to reveal the basic truth about that life, it may have to reject the claims of particular social, ethical, or religious ideals, or even those of Beauty, "the swerga of the aesthete."[13] On the other hand, he clearly does not yet grasp what "truth" means in this context, or how the substance of life is related to its accidents, or even what formal and technical problems confront an art devoted to "truth."

A closely-related limitation appears in his other writings about this time: in his first published article, "Ibsen's New Drama,"[14] which was a review of *When We Dead Awaken* for *The Fortnightly Review* (1 Apr. 1900)—an impressive performance for a youth of eighteen (as Joyce was among the first to recognise); in "The Day of the Rabblement" (1901),[15] which attacked the nationalistic policy of the Irish Literary Theatre; and in the carefully-pondered letter (March 1901) in which he replied to Ibsen's thanks for the earlier review.[16] In all of these Joyce touches on the artist's own attitudes—to his world on the one hand and to his work on the other—and in each case he oversimplifies the problems involved. He shows no real appreciation of Ibsen's own vital engagement in his art, much less of the complex and difficult impersonality he achieved in it. Believing that the "truth" about humanity can be seen only from a position somewhere beyond its particular social manifestations, he supposes that Ibsen's impersonality consisted in "the wilful resolution to wrest the secret from life," the "absolute indifference to public canons of art, friends, and shibboleths." He calls it an "inward heroism"; what he really means and admires, however, is the dubious "objectivity" of a socially alienated, independent, and determined will. It is hardly surprising that in 1900 he wrote a play in imitation of Ibsen called *A Brilliant Career*, which he solemnly dedicated "To My own Soul";[17] in 1902 he tore it up.

In 1902 he was ready to deliver another paper to the same college society, this time on the Irish poet James Clarence Mangan.[18] By now he was evidently rather more critical of Romanticism and beginning to face some

been something of a commonplace at least since Kant:
the "purposiveness without purpose" characteristic of
art. On the other hand, Joyce's early formulation of the
idea involves certain difficulties. He is, for instance, in
some danger of cutting art off from ordinary human
feelings altogether and so divorcing it from *any* moral
significance. Equally, he fails to see how the "beauty" of
art and its "truth" are interconnected. We judge the
moral significance of a work, call it "true" or "profound," not according to the "changeless laws" it
exposes or its mere subject-matter, but according to the
depth of its imaginative presentment of life. Artistic
"truth" is not a mere accompaniment of "beauty," nor
are they separable qualities. At this stage, Joyce seems to
have thought they were: "the most satisfying relations of
the intelligible" was truth; "the most satisfying relations
of the sensible" was beauty; and art somehow put them
together in the "disposition of sensible or intelligible
matter for an aesthetic end."[23]

As Joyce himself was to show in *Ulysses*, this oversimplified the crucial function of the artist's medium,
and, even more, oversimplified the nature of the artist's
own impersonality. But it also raised a question that the
young Joyce did see needed an immediate answer: how
is it that the *stasis* of good art (its "aesthetic end") pro-
vides an imaginative *illumination of life* as well as the
satisfaction of certain special feelings? His answer was to
analyse the act of apprehension and to try to show that,
as we come to *see* truth, so we come to *feel* emotional
stasis. He was at last face to face with his crucial problem
—but of course he could not solve it.

The theory of "epiphany" in *Stephen Hero* is this
attempt. He started with a sentence, taken out of context, from Aquinas: "the three things requisite for
beauty are, integrity, . . . symmetry, and radiance,"
the three qualities that in the later *Portrait* are given in
Latin: *integritas*, *consonantia*, and *claritas*.[24] As he also

assumed in his notebooks, these would produce the requisite *emotional stasis*; he had to show how they correspond to the stages of perceiving *truth*. First, he argued, we perceive *integritas*, the object as a separate thing. Then symmetry or *consonantia*—the object's structure. Finally,

> when the relation of the parts is exquisite, when the parts are adjusted to the special point, we recognise that it is *that* thing which it is. Its soul, its whatness, leaps to us from the vestment of its appearance. The soul of the commonest object, the structure of which is so adjusted, seems to us radiant. The object achieves its epiphany.[25]

This is a brave attempt, but it is hardly satisfactory. The model that Stephen (and Joyce) have in mind for the artist is still the scientific observer, armed now with a special optical instrument: "the gropings of a spiritual eye which seeks to adjust its vision to an exact focus."[26] The "truth" is thought of as something given, objectively presented to an "indifferent" observer; art is thought of as the mere representation of what is observed. Joyce has not realised that the artist creates more than a "truth"-telling object, that in fact his "truth" is of a special kind, that "classicism" requires him to understand himself in order to understand what he sees, and that his understanding must ultimately affect the very form and language of his work. Joyce's own "epiphanies," written between 1900 and 1903, reinforce the point.[27] They are sharp, economical fragments, but they are so *de*personalised in their "objectivity" that they end up with a merely subjective significance.

As always, his attitudes to art were an inseparable part of his life. No less than his writings, his actions over this period betray the same immaturity, the same unsophisticated belief that Truth is simply there for those with eyes to see, and the same unconscious projection of his own feelings into the external world, so that fact and interpretation, fate and choice, object and subject, become hopelessly confused. Stanislaus mentions his brother's early "heroic" determination to make his life "an experiment in living," to be "the deliberate artificer" of his "own style of life";[28] and during these years we can recognise the limitations of his youthful style. Richard Ellmann's encyclopaedic biography of Joyce makes the revealing, and sometimes comic, pattern quite clear.[29] Having declared his rejection of current values all through his university days, and graduating B.A. in 1902, Joyce now found himself satisfactorily at odds with his environment. Lack of money, lack of a career, lack of what he thought sufficient respect for his talents and his aesthetic views, enabled him to cultivate a sense of persecution befitting his status as an Ibsenite "artist." Life *had* to provide him with opportunities for heroic "indifference to public canons of art, friends, and shibboleths"; whenever it seemed likely to fail him, he employed the talent, which he never lost, of nudging fate in the direction he thought it should make him go. "He had come to the conclusion," he wrote,[30] "that nature had designed him for a man of letters and therefore he determined that, in spite of all influences, he would do as nature counselled"; and he saw to it that "nature" would make him exactly the kind of man of letters he wanted to become.

Thus in 1902 he found himself equipped with enough hostility and heroism to undertake his first "exile" from Dublin—a few weeks in Paris (which in the *Portrait* he conflated with his departure two years later). He was recalled by the news of his mother's dying, and during the next two years he spent his time writing a few poems, earning a little with reviews, drinking and roistering, collecting various snubs, and beginning what were eventually to be *Dubliners*, *Chamber Music*, and *Stephen Hero*. He considered and rejected a career as a singer. He began to work out the theory about Hamlet mentioned in *Ulysses*. And in 1904 he met Nora Barnacle, fell immediately in love with her, and persuaded her to throw in her lot with him when he left Dublin a few months later on his second, more serious, exile.

In all of this, as Ellmann shows, Joyce at least half-provoked the spiting influences he needed for his self-image. And, of course, once he began to write about himself, he soon found that he could shape his work as he wanted only if his life followed the pattern of his aesthetic assumptions: a full-scale "exile" had become both an artistic and a personal necessity. To some extent he did grow rather more aware of what he was doing: he did, for instance, "accept" his "*voluntary* exile" because it would provide him with suitable material for his novel.[31] On the other hand, his self-awareness was still far from complete. He was also convinced, for instance, that his former friends had betrayed him to the "martyrdom" of exile and had done so simply in order to maintain the conventional values against which he had pitted his own "moral nature."[32] Years later he was still complaining about the problems involved "when your work and life make one, when they are interwoven in the same fabric"[33]—the difficulty of "organizing" an artist's career.[34] For Joyce life and art, fact and feeling, were never widely separate; nevertheless, he had to learn to distinguish them before he could confuse them deliberately, and therefore meaningfully, in his work.

But in 1904 he was still very much the alienated young "artist," and it was in this temper of social rejection and personal vindication that he conceived *Dubliners* and *Stephen Hero*. The one was "to betray the soul of that hemiplegia or paralysis" he thought characteristic of Dublin;[35] the other was to define the constant traits of his own character and their "reactions to hereditary influences and environment."[36] Not unnaturally, he looked for some relief from this stern programme and found it in poetry. *Chamber Music*, he said later, was written "as a protest against myself"[37]—a comment that helps to explain why the poems were generally acceptable at the time and why they are comparatively negligible as poetry. Indeed, even the broadside he wrote in 1904, "The Holy Office," has more life in it—largely because it is so charged with the spirited defiance with which his early prose was written and with which he left Dublin:

> I stand the self-doomed, unafraid,
> Unfellowed, friendless and alone,
> Indifferent as the herring-bone,
> Firm as the mountain-ridges where
> I flash my antlers on the air. . . .
> And though they spurn me from their door
> My soul shall spurn them evermore.[38]

As he himself wished, his departure does conveniently mark the end of one stage of his life. The next ends with the abandonment of *Stephen Hero* and the consequent birth of *A Portrait of the Artist as a Young Man* and the conception of *Ulysses* as its sequel: the crucial period of growth between 1904 and 1906–7.

Joyce's "voluntary exile" took him first to Zürich, then to Pola, then in 1905 to Trieste. He supported himself by teaching English at the Berlitz School while he continued the stories and the novel he had already begun, determined, as he said, to "sharpen that little pen and dip it into fermented ink and write tiny little sentences about the people who betrayed me."[39] He finished *Dubliners* in 1905 (and began the nine-year struggle to find a publisher willing to print it). As soon as he had finished the book, however, he began to feel an uneasiness, a significant doubt about the spirit in which it was written: was it not perhaps a caricature of Dublin? Was his spirit merely "mischievous"? His brother Stanislaus reassured him; soon he was assuring himself by checking that all the details in the stories were accurate; and he ended by persuading himself, and trying to persuade others, that the "style of scrupulous meanness" and the "special odour of corruption" he had achieved would have a morally liberating effect on his country.[40] *Dubliners* would let in fresh air; "it is not my fault," he wrote to a recalcitrant publisher, "that the odour of ashpits and old weeds and offal hangs round my stories. I seriously believe that you will retard the course of civilization in Ireland by preventing the Irish people from having one good look at themselves in my nicely-polished looking-glass."[41]

Two years later he was less content merely to echo his earlier attitudes. The doubts returned; by 1907 his attitude to Ireland had changed and with it his attitude to his work: "sometimes thinking of Ireland it seems to me that I have been unnecessarily harsh. I have repro-duced (in *Dubliners* at least) none of the attraction of the city . . . its ingenuous insularity and its hospitality . . . its beauty. . . ."[42] In this mood he conceived a new story with which to end the book: "The Dead," by far the most subtle and the most moving story in it. Another significant sign was his attitude to his poems, now about to be published as *Chamber Music*: it was, he said, "a young man's book," and he wanted a title for it "which to a certain extent repudiated the book, without alto-gether disparaging it."[43] The same soon applied to his view of himself. *Stephen Hero* became bogged down; Joyce restlessly moved from Trieste to Rome and then back again; he began to feel himself that he was changing: "I have certain ideas I would like to give form to: not as a doctrine but as a continuation of the expression of myself which I now see I began in *Chamber Music*. These ideas or instincts or intuitions or impulses may be purely personal. . . ."[44] The self-awareness, the hesitant tone are new. Some lectures he gave in Trieste in 1907 show the same drift: his view of Ireland and of James Clarence Mangan are less "heroic," less solipsistic, more truly objective.[45] Finally, in the latter months of 1907, he completed "The Dead" and decided to rewrite *Stephen Hero* completely. By the end of that year, the *Portrait* was under way, and he was thinking of expanding an abandoned short story, "Ulysses," into a book. He had, so to speak, artistically come of age.

Of all his novels, *Stephen Hero* gives the most accurate account of what the young Joyce's attitudes really were: the moral intransigence, the stress on "truth"-telling in art, "classicism," the "epiphany"—all these represent the facts accurately enough. In both the *Portrait* and *Ulysses*, however, he changed the facts in order to express a deeper understanding of his own history; specifically, he heightened the immaturity of the younger Stephen in the *Portrait* and the access of wisdom visible in *Ulysses*. The ideas he gives Stephen in the *Portrait*, for example, include none of the young Joyce's own ideas about the moral and social significance of art, and they contain nothing of his belief that the stable, humane "joy" of comedy is ultimately "the perfect manner in art."[46] Instead, Stephen sees art only in terms of Beauty, and the more closely we inspect his attitudes the more clearly he appears limited by his aestheticism. But Joyce had now come to see that Stephen's discovery that art has moral and social dimensions was a crucial part of his growth; and so he holds that discovery back until Stephen is ripe for it—in *Ulysses*. Hence the paradox that *Ulysses* harks back to some of the attitudes of *Stephen Hero* more clearly than does the *Portrait*; but now those attitudes are given a form more sophisticated, and more satisfactory, than Joyce had been able to give them himself in 1904. But if *Ulysses* distorts the historical facts of the past, it is true to those of the present. It is *Ulysses* that expresses Joyce's mature conception of his art, the outlook characteristic of this next period of his life—from about 1907 to about 1920, when *Ulysses* was nearing completion. Stephen's speculations in *Ulysses*—on art, on time, on *Hamlet* and Shakespeare—reflect the insight of the mature Joyce, who could now portray the image of his younger "self" reaching towards ideas that his present self, the author of the *Portrait* and *Ulysses*, commanded so firmly that he could embody them in the very works in which he portrayed that earlier self.

We might define that maturity as a deepening of his whole conception of "drama," the term with which he began. All his early ideas are summed up in the grandiloquent words he gives Stephen in the *Portrait*:

> The personality of the artist, at first a cry or a cadence or a mood and then a fluid and lambent narrative, finally refines itself out of existence, impersonalises itself, so to speak. The esthetic image in the dramatic form is life purified in and reprojected from the human imagination. The mystery of esthetic, like that of material creation, is accomplished. The artist, like the God of creation, remains within or behind or beyond or above his handiwork, invisible, refined out of existence, indifferent, paring his fingernails.[47]

The grandiloquence (and, as we shall see, the dramatic context) of this deliberately underline its limitations. For the artist to "refine himself out of existence" requires a harder kind of discipline than the young Stephen or the young Joyce had imagined, and his "indifference" is of a rather different kind.

The maturer ideas in *Ulysses* are expounded in a complicated and fragmentary way, but we can sum them up in a number of propositions.[48] In the first place, Stephen is now made to see *why* the discipline of "classicism" is necessary: no one can ever apprehend the forming "spirit," the inner "drama," of life directly, but only as he apprehends everything else—as it is embodied in the given concrete particulars of "the now, the here," in "what you damn well have to see,"[49] in the society you "damn well" have to live in and understand. Like other men, the artist is necessarily part of that "now and here."

Whether he likes it or not, he lives in his age and his age lives in him. Shakespeare, for example, was a representative Elizabethan as well as a supreme dramatic artist;[50] it is significant that now Joyce makes the somewhat wiser Stephen take Shakespeare, not Ibsen, as his exemplar.

In the second place, Stephen is now made to concentrate less on the ambiguous term "epiphany" and more on the artist's "word."[51] That "word," as he is now made to see, is like the Word of God in that it expresses a meaning born in the union of the knower and the known in the act of understanding. Like God in relation to the world, the artist *creates* his imaginative world—his characters, his setting, his plot, and so on—out of himself, even as (in another sense) he *finds* it in the external world he has experienced. What he "feels" becomes one with what he "sees"; value is objectified; fact is made meaningful. Thus Shakespeare "found in the world without as actual what was in his world within as possible. . . . We walk through ourselves, meeting robbers, ghosts, giants, old men, young men, wives, widows, brothers-in-love. But always meeting ourselves."[52] And yet "all events brought grist to his mill"—every aspect of his plays reflects the world without.[53]

A third implication of this line of thought is even more obviously relevant to Joyce's achievement in both the *Portrait* and *Ulysses*: that life is fulfilled most completely in the reflexive act wherein it understands itself. The living mind seeks its end in the knowledge of what it has become through its successive acts of understanding and its consequent acts of will (as Joyce sought to know himself in understanding the process of Stephen's growth). The fullest life of the spirit is achieved when (like God) it *comprehends* its whole experience—including its present act of understanding. Here, obviously, is the rationale of an autobiographical art, of an artistic "word" that expresses, not the merely chronological sequence of the artist's activities, but their inner drama, their implicit form and significance. In tracing the "slow and dark birth" of the self[54]—the "everchanging forms" of the soul, "entelechy, form of forms," which abides through its memories[55]—the artist is able to profit from his experience. For a man of genius, Stephen argues, even his past errors are in a sense "volitional," the means to finding himself, "portals of discovery."[56]

Thus a fully autobiographical art would most purely express the artist's understanding of life as he actually knew it, including his understanding of his own present activity as an artist. It would be an account of his world and at the same time of himself: the ultimate condition of artistic "truth." Stephen interprets *Hamlet* as Shakespeare's crucial act of autobiographical understanding in this sense; but more importantly, he obviously looks forward to a similar achievement himself:

—As we, or mother Dana, weave and unweave our bodies, Stephen said, from day to day, their molecules shuttled to and fro, so does the artist weave and unweave his image. And as the mole on my right breast is where it is when I was born, though all my body has been woven of new stuff time after time, so through the ghost of the unquiet father the image of the unliving son looks forth. In the intense instant of imagination, when the mind, Shelley says, is a fading coal, that which I was is that which I am and that which in possibility I may come to be. So in the future, the sister of the past, I may see myself as I sit here now but by reflection from that which then I shall be.[57]

Stephen now applies his terms, *kinesis* and *stasis*, to a more valuable distinction than that simply between supposedly different sorts of emotion. He now sees that the terms apply more properly to different conditions of the whole personality: on the one hand, to the immaturity that can only *react* subjectively to the external world, and

on the other, to the maturity that can *understand and value*
the world objectively. For the relationship between the
younger, immature personality and the older, more
balanced one, able to judge and to act rationally because
it knows itself and others, he now uses the metaphor of
"fatherhood." He derives it partly from Shakespeare's
particular case, partly from the analogy between the
artist and God. The artist's understanding of himself
when young, an understanding expressed in the portrait
of himself as a young man, is the act of understanding
that makes him a man, a father. The fictional child becomes, as it were, father to the man, but the father is also
himself his own son.[58]

All this applies to any man, however, not just the
artist. Indeed, the artist, as Joyce now sees, is simply a
man like others, but one whose vocation requires of him
a more disciplined, more articulate moral consciousness.
Every man—even a humble, limited commercial traveller
like Leopold Bloom in the Dublin of 1904—tries to
understand his experience; Joyce's so-called "stream-of-
consciousness" in *Ulysses* is in fact the portrayal of Bloom's
acts of understanding, his "word." And Bloom has one
great advantage over Stephen: although Stephen knows
theoretically what he must try to achieve, he is still too
kinetically involved in his world, still too much merely
reactive, to achieve the freedom of detached, impersonal
understanding of it. In this at least he does embody
Joyce's understanding of what he himself was in 1904 and
also the moral liberation from that nightmare which
Joyce's understanding brought with it. Bloom, on the
other hand, is a maturer man even though a far more
limited one: and in his maturity, at least, he represents
the later Joyce. His maturity and his very ordinariness—
both of which represent the world Stephen must yet
experience—make him, metaphorically, the "father" of
Stephen. But of course both characters are only partial
aspects of a third figure who found them within himself

as well as in the world without: Joyce. Like Shakespeare in Stephen's theory, Joyce comprehends Stephen and Bloom in his self-understanding, in the "word" which is *Ulysses* itself.

Thus Joyce found the essential "drama" he had to portray was not independent of the actors or the accidents of time and place, and involved him within his handiwork as a condition of his refining himself out of it. He had, like other men, to traverse the world about him in order to discover and become the self which, as Stephen puts it, he was "ineluctably preconditioned to become."[59] Seeing the need of this meant he had to comprehend all the scattered efforts of his earlier works. It meant reconsidering his own past and the Dublin he knew in his formative years, rethinking his aesthetic position, reimagining both *Dubliners* and *Stephen Hero*.[60] He found his "drama" in the process of his own maturation as the human being he was at a particular now and here; coming to awareness, he was a man like any other, but one who could perhaps express the universal drama his life embodied. Hence the peculiar nature of the *Portrait* and *Ulysses* as works that take themselves as symbolic of the moral vitality which is their real subject, and explore the wider significance of the particular self and the particular world they each portray. They focus life in the problem of art, and specifically in their own art, their own conditions of achievement, and the ambiguous process of time which (as they portray it) binds humanity to its accidental circumstances, and yet (as they fulfil it) may also lead humanity to the freedom of understanding and fulfilment in rationally chosen action.

Exactly how long it took Joyce to formulate these attitudes we do not know, but he was at work on the *Portrait* between early 1907 and early 1915, on his play, *Exiles*, between 1913 and 1915, and on *Ulysses* between 1914 and 1922; and all seem to spring from the same basic outlook as the theory in *Ulysses*. It is an outlook that

went with the other changes in Joyce during these years.
As well as the self-critical craftsman, he was now something of a family-man, a not unsuccessful teacher, a
shrewd (but not successful) businessman, a "socialist,"
even a journalist. His circle of friends grew; he was
usually well enough off not to have to divert too much
time from his real work; and from 1917 on he attracted
some very generous patronage. He was still the same
Joyce, of course: quick to see conspiracies against him,
demanding implicit faith from his friends, using (and
half-provoking) fact to serve his fiction—as when he
exploited his own jealousy of Nora for "The Dead,"
Exiles, and *Ulysses*—and still, beneath the daily surface
of his life, utterly dedicated to the incessant, meticulous
demands of his art. But he knew himself far better now,
and could treat his jealousy or his complaints or his
demands on others with humorous detachment even
while he persisted in them. His life at this time reveals a
vigorous, concentrated energy that survived every
frustrating circumstance—and there were enough of
those. The outbreak of World War I drove him from
Trieste to Zürich, and it was there that he wrote the
greater part of *Ulysses*. In 1919 he returned to Trieste; in
the following year he moved again, this time to Paris,
where he completed *Ulysses* and was to remain until
World War II drove him back finally to Zürich. He
finally succeeded in getting *Dubliners* published in 1914,
the *Portrait* in 1916, and *Ulysses* in 1922, and in each case
there was a notable battle with Mrs Grundy. But the
publication of *Ulysses* really marked the end of this period
of his life. From then on his work was increasingly
known, denounced, and praised; his reputation kept on
growing as *Ulysses* became available first in France, then
in the U.S.A. and other countries, and then even in
England, and critical discussion about him swelled into a
flood. It was with a circle of friendly admirers about him
that he began the last of his books—the labour that was

to occupy him, in the midst of severe eye-troubles, the private distress of his daughter's insanity, and the ominous public events of the late nineteen-twenties and -thirties, for sixteen years. In 1939 his "Work in Progress" was finally completed and published as *Finnegans Wake*.

What we make of his attitudes over this last period of his life, from about 1922 to his death in 1941, largely depends on what we make of *Finnegans Wake*. To many, this is the time of his supreme mastery, when his impersonal manner, enabling him to withdraw his imagination from notoriety and distraction and pain, reached its fruition in the triumphantly impersonal "drama" of *Finnegans Wake*. To me, I must confess, Joyce's letters, memoirs of him, and Richard Ellmann's detailed record, like *Finnegans Wake* itself, leave an impression of a slackening rather than any heightening of vitality. The tensions between the man who suffered and the mind which created, which were so fruitful in the years between 1907 and 1922, seem to lapse; the gap between them now appears to grow wider; or rather there now seems to be no real effort needed to keep them separate, no busy spiritual traffic in the gap. It is as if Joyce's imagination relaxed after the long-gestated fulfilment of *Ulysses* and, in doing so, resumed some of the aspirations of his early youth, as if he now no longer recognised the need for the hard discipline of confronting the world in *its* terms. As *Ulysses* came to completion and in the years of *Finnegans Wake*, his attention seems to have retreated from actuality to the private devotion of "art" and particularly to its technical problems. In 1936 he said that "since 1922 my book has been a greater reality for me than reality,"[61] and his whole conception of *Finnegans Wake* betrays the same abstracted condition. It returns to his first idea of "drama": its subject would be the strife, the evolution of humanity as a whole, the "spirit" coeval with life itself. In order to portray it he had to turn from the world of consciousness, of ordinary realities, to what he called "the esthetic of the dream, where the forms prolong and multiply themselves, where the visions pass from the trivial to the apocalyptic, where the brain uses the roots of vocables to make others from them which will be capable of naming its phantasms, its allegories, its allusions."[62] In other words, he now sought "drama" in the most basic acts of the mind, in the most elemental patterns it creates-and-finds in its experience even before it is conscious of it *as* experience, where the archetypes of our "subjective" life coalesce with the recurrent patterns of "objective" history.[63] Language itself had therefore to be refashioned in order to reveal, beneath the words of particular languages, the basic nature of language itself as the "word" of a universal process;[64] and for the same reason, the accidents of every time and every place had to be fused together, the experience of a Dublin family reduced to its basic elements ("man and woman, birth, childhood, night, sleep, marriage, prayer, death"), humanity itself had to merge with even more elemental heroes, "time and the river and the mountain,"[65] and the only artistic form able to contain all this was an elaborate, extrinsic arrangement inspired by the Book of Kells.[66] It was a grandiose scheme, and the impulse behind was undoubtedly a genuine desire to take his conception of human "drama" to its ultimate conclusion. But its conclusion brought him, paradoxically, to something like its dubious beginnings; and we may wonder how far the cathartic fulfilment of *Ulysses* released his earliest desire for a heroic, unconditioned artistic freedom ("I have discovered I can do anything with language I want"),[67] and an unslaked ambition, partly egotistic but perhaps partly carried over from the Symbolists of his youth: "I'd like a language which is above all languages, a language to which all will do service. I cannot express myself in English without enclosing myself in a tradition."[68]

As "Work in Progress" appeared in *transition*, the opposition it met made Joyce defensive about it, and as with *Dubliners* he began to feel some doubt himself. Was he, he wondered, "on the wrong track"?[69] Unfortunately, the only kind of doubt he took any notice of was secondary, not fundamental: the book's obscurity, for instance, or its apparent lack of purpose. To both of these he soon had an answer, but one that hardly touched the issue underlying both. For the basic questions are those raised by his own theory in *Ulysses*: how can any artist—a particular man in a particular "now and here"—apprehend *all* human experience directly? In what relevant sense of the word can the meaning, the "drama," of the whole of human life be *imagined*? Stanislaus, with his usual shrewdness, had already commented on Joyce's tendency in some of the later episodes of *Ulysses* to "try to tell every damn thing you know about anybody that appears or anything that crops up";[70] Joyce himself confessed, though evidently without realising the further implications of his criticism, that he "may have over systematized *Ulysses*";[71] and Ezra Pound came close to the point again when he wrote to Joyce about "Work in Progress" that "nothing would be worth plowing through like this, except the Divine Vision—and I gather it's not that sort of thing."[72] Joyce, however, rather thought it was,[73] and he tended to silence doubt by explaining that the obscurity was that of night-experience; that anyway it was "all so simple. If anyone doesn't understand a passage, all he need do is read it aloud";[74] that he was too original for Academicians to understand;[75] that his obscurity was different from others' because he could justify every line of his book;[76] that the "music" of his writing was more important than the meaning (a belief he certainly acted on when it was being translated);[77] that his book was not meaningless, for he had put so much time and labour and erudition into it.[78] In short, complexity tended to become identified with complication,

c

and the value of the work with his willed devotion to it—
so much so, indeed, that he could joke about keeping the
critics busy for three hundred years or demanding of the
reader the devotion of a lifetime to his works. He rewrote
and polished the well-known section, "Anna Livia
Plurabelle," in order to refute his critics, and up to a
point it did so;[79] whether it refuted the relevant criticisms, and whether this section is typical of the whole,
are different questions. But one of his remarks at least is
obviously true: the book *is* conceived in a spirit, however
ambiguous, of comic "joy"; "it's meant," he once said,
"to make you laugh,"[80] and some of the best parts of it
are those that do.

The publication of *Finnegans Wake* left Joyce empty and
exhausted—"I've tried everything"—but his personal
troubles, illness, and the outbreak of war allowed him no
recovery. In 1940 he returned to Zürich, where he had
first gone in his "exile" with Nora in 1904, where he had
written most of *Ulysses*, and where he was now to die.
He was always superstitious—about thunder, dogs, his
birthday, about everything even down to the date—and
he often went to enormous pains to satisfy his superstitious feelings: the publication of his books, for example,
was carefully arranged so that fate should be *made*
auspicious, life subtly directed to make him do what he
wanted it to make him do, just as in his books he reshaped
life as he felt he had to in order to make it yield, as
fiction, the truth he had felt. Indeed, the interwoven
threads of fact and feeling, objective fate and subjective
desire, truth and fiction, made the fabric of his whole
life; and no one, we can be sure, would have enjoyed the
subtle coincidence of his death in Zürich more than he.

REFERENCES

1. E., p. 551. Ellmann's biography of Joyce supersedes Herbert Gorman's *James Joyce* (1940, 1948). However, I have restricted references to E mainly for quotations from Joyce (and others) to be found in it.
2. Cp. *M.B.K.*, p. 53; *L.*, p. 52.
3. *P.*, p. 251 (291).
4. Cp. *L.*, p. 166; *M.B.K.*, pp. 186–7, 189.
5. *M.B.K.*, p. 116.
6. *Op. cit.*, pp. 160, 163 ff. Cp. E., pp. 410, 578.
7. *C.W.*, p. 161.
8. Cp. *M.B.K.*, p. 120; E., pp. 27, 28, 129, 142.
9. E., p. 47.
10. E., pp. 51 ff; *M.B.K.*, pp. 104 ff.
11. *C.W.*, pp. 38–46; E., pp. 72 ff.
12. *C.W.*, pp. 40–1.
13. *Op. cit.*, p. 43.
14. *Op. cit.*, pp. 47–67.
15. *Op. cit.*, pp. 68–72.
16. *L.*, pp. 51–2.
17. E., pp. 81 ff.
18. *C.W.*, pp. 73–83.
19. *Op. cit.*, pp. 101, 104.
20. For his earliest conception of "epiphany," see *M.B.K.*, p. 134.
21. *C.W.*, pp. 143–6.
22. *P.*, pp. 209 ff. (240 ff.).
23. *C.W.*, pp. 145–8; *S.H.*, pp. 175–6 (170–1).
24. *P.*, p. 216 (248).
25. *S.H.*, p. 218 (213).
26. *Op. cit.*, p. 216 (211).
27. See *Epiphanies*, ed. O. A. Silverman, University of Buffalo 1956.
28. *M.B.K.*, pp. 120–1, 171.
29. *E.g.* E., pp. 94, 110–11, 113–114, 120, 154, 189.
30. *S.H.*, p. 213 (208).
31. E., p. 201.
32. *Op. cit.*, p. 207.
33. *Op. cit.*, p. 154.
34. Maria Jolas, "Joyce's friend Jolas," in *J.J.M.*, p. 73.
35. E., p. 169.
36. *M.B.K.*, p. 39.
37. E., pp. 154–5. Cp. *M.B.K.*, p. 150.
38. *C.W.*, p. 152.
39. E., p. 208.
40. *Op. cit.*, pp. 216–18.
41. *L.*, pp. 63–4.
42. E., p. 239.
43. *Op. cit.*, p. 241.
44. *Op. cit.*, p. 249.
45. *C.W.*, pp. 153–86.
46. *Op. cit.*, p. 144.
47. *P.*, p. 219 (252).
48. For a fuller analysis of Joyce's aesthetic, see S. L. Goldberg, *The Classical Temper*, London 1961, chs. 2–3.
49. *U.*, p. 175 (238; 184).
50. *Op. cit.*, pp. 189–90 (258; 198–9), 193 (262–3; 202).
51. *Op. cit.*, p. 374 (511; 385).
52. *Op. cit.*, p. 201 (273; 210).
53. *Op. cit.*, p. 193 (262; 202).
54. *P.*, p. 207 (238).
55. *U.*, p. 178 (242; 187).
56. *Op. cit.*, p. 179 (243; 188).
57. *Op. cit.*, p. 183 (249; 192).
58. *Op. cit.*, p. 196 (267; 205).

59. *Op. cit.*, p. 479 (623; 494).
60. Cp. E., pp. 367 ff.
61. E., p. 708.
62. *Op. cit.*, p. 559.
63. *Op. cit.*, p. 565.
64. *Op. cit.*, p. 559.
65. *Op. cit.*, pp. 565–6.
66. *Op. cit.*, pp. 558–9.
67. *Op. cit.*, p. 715.
68. *Op. cit.*, p. 410.
69. *Op. cit.*, p. 603. Cp. L., pp. 249, 258, 281.
70. E., p. 590.
71. *Op. cit.*, p. 715.
72. *Op. cit.*, p. 597.
73. *Op. cit.*, p. 721; *F.W.*, p. 611.
74. E., p. 603.
75. *Op. cit.*, p. 626.
76. *Op. cit.*, p. 715.
77. *Op. cit.*, pp. 715, 646, 713.
78. *Op. cit.*, p. 610.
79. *Op. cit.*, p. 727. Cp. L., p. 260.
80. E., p. 716.

CHAPTER II

THE DEVELOPMENT OF THE ART:
CHAMBER MUSIC TO *DUBLINERS*

Provided with a sense of artistic vocation, a medley of vague but Romantic emotions, and a handy readiness to learn quickly, the youthful Joyce first set out, around the turn of the century, to be a poet. *Chamber Music* (1907) preserves the best results of that attempt; the later poems —*Pomes Penyeach* (1927) and "Ecce Puer" (written 1932) —were only slight personal asides from what was by then clearly his main work in prose.

As *Stephen Hero* reveals, the impulse behind his earliest poems was twofold. Rejecting the debased language of the market-place, Joyce sought to attach himself to what he called "the literary tradition": to use the language with the craftsmanly devotion of a "man of letters."[1] On the other hand, adolescence, revolt, Romantic literature, and the isolation he proclaimed as "the first principle of artistic economy," stimulated moods of frustrated longing for "the unknown," "sweet sinkings of consciousness,"[2] and other feelings suitable for poetry. As we might expect, the first efforts were feeble expirations of Byron, Shelley, Pater and the 'nineties, verses all too "romantic" in Stephen Hero's sense—bred of "an insecure, unsatisfied, impatient temper which sees no fit abode here for its ideals and chooses therefore to behold them under insensible figures."[3] Like Stephen, Joyce soon destroyed most of his earliest efforts as "romantic";[4] instead, it seems, he turned to those in which "a mature and seasoned emotion urged him," and in which a sense of the realistic "modern spirit" led him to employ the "feudal" language of his love "a little ironically."[5] He now sought a poetry suggestive, musical, and "ironic"; he cultivated Verlaine and Rimbaud and Elizabethan lyrics and folk-songs; his verse became both more competent and slightly tougher,[6] and *Chamber Music* was the result. But "romanticism" was not to be purged by simply taking thought. Although it was less obvious, it still flourished under the "ironic" shell, and indeed penetrated the shell itself. Most of *Chamber Music*, it is worth recalling, was written by a youth barely in his twenties and in an environment dominated by the art of singing.

Some critics have advanced larger claims for the book: that it is an oblique, "symbolic" treatment of real personal issues, for example,[7] or that it achieves an ironic self-awareness and at times even "a Jonsonian precision and elegance."[8] Even its admirers, however, are forced in the end to recognise the uncertainty, indeed the frailty, of the poet's attitude to the emotions that are his subject, a weakness that really undercuts all such claims. The general verdict is obviously right: despite its possibilities, there is not much to be said for *Chamber Music* as poetry. Occasional poems achieve a certain fragile success (*e.g.*, II, XXXV, XXXVI), but most are mere poeticising in an outworn poetical fashion or pervaded by sentimentality. The "love" seems as factitious as the language. The emotions are jejune; the tone is portentous with "suggestions"; the "symbolism" is at once vague and rather crude; and in the end, the self-conscious "craftsmanship" amounts to little more than cadenced preciosity. To some extent, of course, Joyce does try to distance "emotion" with "irony"—in IV and XII, for instance, by a touch of brisker realism or a conscious ambiguity; or by a "Jonsonian" toughness (as in XXIV and XXVII); or by "modern" disillusionment (XXVIII, XXX)—yet the "irony" is no more convincing, no less self-indulgent, than the sentimental "love." The reason is obvious enough in the directly personal poems (XVII–XIX, XXI–XXII). Although the tight-mouthed rhetoric (the "precision") is here more energetic than the general "love and laughter self-confessed | When the heart is heaviest," the "irony" tends to wobble uncertainly between self-criticism and self-admiration.[9]

Even to mention the name of Jonson is perhaps enough to see how limiting was Joyce's early conception of "the literary tradition" as an inviolate purity of language, a literary craft divorced from the debasements of the market-place.[10] Jonson's precision, urbanity, and elegance are solidly rooted in a real personal maturity and in the realities of the market-place; Eliot, we recall, looked to the Jacobeans too. To apply a phrase from Jonson to *Chamber Music* is to criticise more than Joyce's diction: "in affecting the ancients he writ no language." The best Joyce could yet do were poems like xxxv and xxxvi: unequivocally personal, and achieving a relatively firm (if simple) metaphorical statement. Factitious "irony" and "maturity" give place to a young man's limited, but genuine enough, self-concern.

Pomes Penyeach, however, shows that even later Joyce could not detach—or engage—his imagination sufficiently to create verse of much value. The later poems are firmer and the self-awareness deeper (though the emotions are no less equivocal); but Ezra Pound's judgment in 1927 is clearly right: "they belong in the Bible or in the family album with the portraits."[11] Joyce was never vitally engaged in poetry. The same easy, sentimental "lyricism," the same wobbling "ironies," continued to disturb even his prose works after *Chamber Music*; but there, and only there, he could hope to discipline them by a "classical" devotion to "present things." From his first autobiographical sketch, "A Portrait of the Artist," which he wrote in 1904, through *Stephen Hero*, to *Dubliners*, he sought a style steady enough to focus everything he wanted to say (or could say) in those years—both about the world and about himself.

With the latter subject he failed. The sketch "Portrait,"
for example, slides about between three different styles—
over-elaborately emotional, narcissistic with defensive
flourishes, and (towards the external world) violently
critical. It lacks any stable centre of gravity. Compared
with this naïve rhetoric, the vigour and clarity and
dramatisation of *Stephen Hero*, such as they are, mark a
clear advance. On the other hand, the limited, wavering
emotions and techniques of *Stephen Hero* explain why
Joyce later dismissed it as "puerile," "rubbish."[12]

It was apparently conceived on a large scale, along the
lines of "epical" art as Stephen describes it in the final
Portrait. As the author "prolongs and broods upon himself as the centre of an epical event," his personality no
longer expresses itself directly, but "passes into the
narration itself, flowing round and round the persons and
the action like a vital sea. This progress you will see easily
in that old English ballad *Turpin Hero* which begins in
the first person and ends in the third person."[13] From
report, the early chapters of *Stephen Hero* were lyrical and
nostalgic, the later ones (including those which survive)
realistic and satirical.[14] In these later ones, certainly, the
picture of Stephen and of his world is far more conventionally "realistic" than in the final *Portrait*. The hero
is less an imaginative symbol, the Artist slowly developing
through a series of crucial and representative actions,
than an intelligent, disturbed, lonely, and "heroic"
young student rejecting the values of his provincial,
priest-ridden, conventionally middle-class society.[15] His
family, his friends, his whole social environment get far
more attention than in the *Portrait*. Stephen's criticisms,
too, are diffused far more widely; so indeed is Joyce's
imaginative attention.

But to contrast the "drama" of *Stephen Hero* with the
"soliloquy" of the later *Portrait*, as Harry Levin does, can
be rather misleading.[16] The former includes many
incidents not in the latter, its world is more specifically

detailed, its *technical* point-of-view is ostensibly "objective," and it is less exclusively concerned with Stephen's consciousness. Nevertheless, the dramatic relevance of the detail in *Stephen Hero* is either vague or crudely repetitious, and, more importantly, its *moral* point-of-view is never clearly distinguished from Stephen's own:[17]

As he walked slowly through the maze of poor streets he stared proudly in return for the glances of stupid wonder that he received. . . . These wanderings filled him with deep-seated anger and whenever he encountered a burly black-vested priest taking a stroll of pleasant inspection through these warrens full of swarming and cringing believers he cursed the farce of Irish Catholicism: an island the inhabitants of which entrust their wills and minds to others that they may ensure for themselves a life of spiritual paralysis. . . .

. . . He acknowledged to himself in honest egoism that he could not take to heart the distress of a nation, the soul of which was antipathetic to his own, so bitterly as the indignity of a bad line of verse: but at the same time he was nothing in the world so little as an amateur artist. He wished to express his nature freely and fully for the benefit of a society which he would enrich and also for his own benefit, seeing that it was part of his life to do so. . . .[18]

In its attitude to its material, this is much more like soliloquy than drama. While the book purports to treat its material objectively, even to criticise the hero's outlook, its most explicit "criticisms" are in fact protective, subtle endorsements of his judgment. Thus it is more accurate, historically, than the *Portrait*: even if Joyce sometimes adapted facts to his own purposes in it, its attitudes are really those he himself had between 1900 and 1906.[19] Although it gropes towards the kind of art that arises from "the most stable mood of the mind,"[20] it reveals the unstable moods of immaturity; although the artist is determined that his work will "proceed from a free and noble source" of life,[21] he can see little to portray in the life outside himself except "a hell which would be a caricature of Dante's."[22] Its hero is the author.

This is not to deny the readability and the evident promise of the book. Some of the writing is crisp and at times even witty, though usually when the subject has little to do with Stephen. Many of the scenes are vividly drawn, though the author too often shares his hero's view of the situation more than the reader does. Occasionally he achieves a subtly meaningful juxtaposition of events, though he usually destroys the effect with Stephen's cruder (and rather boring) reflexions upon the event, or allows the transitions to seem merely abrupt and pointless. Again, some of the characters (especially Stephen's family) are treated with a warm, sympathetic understanding, though the understanding is dramatically unused since it never penetrates into the hero's attitudes and Joyce never sees that it ought. Ultimately, the balance tips over; the general effect becomes one of monotonous self-vindication. What purports to *render* Stephen's vision ends by adopting it, just as the occasional phrases that try to place it ("intemperate anger," "fantastic idealist," "ingenuous arrogance," and the like) do nothing to check the current of emotional identification. The contradictions in Stephen are left unfocused. The intelligence that is supposed to be "as much in love with laughter as with combat,"[23] for example, is strikingly shy of both. One crucial inconsistency is simply stated and then ignored: "he took her hand ... caressing also his own past towards which this inconsistent hater of inheritances was always lenient."[24] What starts off with pretensions to a larger "maturity" than Stephen's—"for his part he was at the difficult age, dispossessed and necessitous ..."[25]—

invariably dissolves into vagueness or sentimentality or both.[26]

One interesting passage reveals both the strength and the weakness of the book: the description of three clerks playing billiards in the Adelphi Hotel while Stephen and his friend, Cranly, silently watch them.[27] The style is that of *Dubliners*—cool, clear-eyed, objective, "scrupulously mean," and it renders the episode with precisely the judgment Joyce wants to make upon it. Unfortunately the dramatic context quite undermines the judgment. It is not only that Joyce is crudely explicit— "the hopeless pretence of those three lives before him, their unredeemable servility, made the back of Stephen's eyes feel burning hot. . . . O, hopeless! hopeless! said Stephen clenching his fists."[28] What is much more revealing, Joyce fails to notice that his hero's judgment is deeply compromised. Just before visiting the hotel, Stephen has undergone a long, abusive attack from his father about his "bohemian" life, about *his* futility. He has made no reply—his feelings are left implicit in his silence. Remembering that, however, we start wondering if we do not see more than Joyce. How far is Stephen's judgment of the clerks the suppressed reply to his father's criticism of him? How much is it coloured by his personal frustration? How is his anger different from that of, say, the clerk in "Counterparts" in *Dubliners*, who directs his frustrations upon a helpless object? And how different is Stephen's equivocal judgment from that implicit in *Joyce's* style? To ask these questions is to see how fully the book relies upon our accepting Stephen's essential rightness, on our immediate assent to the values he is constantly proclaiming. And yet it is also to realise how lifeless those values remain—the abstract "heroism" of the unashamed egoist pitting his own "nature," "freedom," "life," "art," "human dignity," and so on, against the pervasive hypocrisy, the materialistic "paralysis" or "simony,"[29] of everyone else: of society. Undoubtedly, Stephen is right in most of his rejections (probably most of Joyce's critics have been drawn to his work partly because, in some sense or other, they share them): but his (and Joyce's own) positive values remain so vague, their alleged "vitality" is so little felt in the writing, that they quite fail to support imaginatively the savage criticisms delivered in their name. The actual force in the writing comes from *kinetic* recoil, rejection. Despite the occasional, uncertain gestures of "maturity," the author's imagination sees life (as his hero does) in relatively crude, black-and-white terms.

The limitations of *Stephen Hero* are obvious enough and it is easy to see why Joyce eventually had to abandon it. But they also explain one of the conditions of his success in *Dubliners*, which was written more or less at the same time and reflects, obliquely, many of the same ideas. For one thing, he had to get rid of Stephen. Joyce's self-knowledge was still too slender for him to portray himself convincingly. But this also meant that he could not yet convincingly portray, specifically, in depth, his central values, what he could feel as genuine vitality of spirit. *Dubliners* succeeds because he found there a way of doing what he *could* do, but the limitations of that are the measure of its achievement.

Whatever influences may be detected in *Dubliners*—and Chekhov, Maupassant, George Moore, and Flaubert have all been mentioned[30]—and however easy it has since become to write the same kind of stories, it is nevertheless a remarkable achievement for a writer in his early twenties. The stories are by no means simple naturalistic sketches, as some have thought them; nor, on the other hand, are they structures of infinitely complex "symbolism."[31] Each brings a limited area of experience to sharp focus, renders visible its "whatness," and does so with an economical, concentrated purposefulness that gives the realistic details their full metaphorical import. Joyce had learned his craft. What is more, the stories are lightly but suggestively related, so that the book is something more than merely a sum of its parts.

The opening sentences of the first story, "The Sisters," as we gradually come to realise, are something like a statement of the major themes of the whole book:

> There was no hope for him this time: it was the third stroke. Night after night I had passed the house (it was vacation time) and studied the lighted square of the window: and night after night I had found it lighted in the same way, faintly and evenly. If he was dead, I thought, I would see the reflection of candles on the darkened blind, for I knew that two candles must be set at the head of a corpse. He had often said to me: 'I am not long for this world,' and I had thought his words idle. Now I knew they were true. Every night as I gazed up at the window I said softly to myself the word paralysis. It had always sounded strangely in my ears, like the word gnomon in the Euclid and the word simony in the Catechism. But now it sounded to me like the name of some maleficent and sinful being. It filled me with fear, and yet I longed to be nearer to it and to look upon its deadly work.

The terms "paralysis" and "simony" (more discursively defined in *Stephen Hero*) suggest the pervasive moral condition, the "maleficent and sinful being," exposed in story after story.[32] "Gnomon" suggests their artistic method, by which the whole is suggested by the part or (as with the gnomon on a sun-dial) the light by its shadow: the simple but effective metaphor of light/darkness is used in many of the stories.

In this first story, the old priest's physical paralysis becomes the mark of his failure of courage before the divine mystery he had tried to serve, and of his consequent resignation to hopelessness and death. In "An Encounter," the paralysis is that of diseased obsession. The unruly, romantic, adventurous spirit of the boy, seeking a larger freedom of life, encounters only the maleficent disorder of the old pervert; yet although he fears it, he outwits it: courage wins him his freedom. In "Araby," the boy's romantic longings at last collapse and yet triumph in the darkened hall of the bazaar; the chink of money and the inane chatter there come to represent the materialistic "simony" which (even in his own desires) at once betrays his foolish ideals and is itself exposed by their innocent "folly." And so on through the book. The stories become images: of paralysed automatism of the will, the paralysing hand of the past, a paralysing feebleness of moral imagination, a simoniacal willingness to buy and sell the life of the spirit, timidity, frustration, self-righteousness, fear of convention, fear of sin, hypocrisy, vulgarity, pettiness. Each, with a fine dexterity, vivisects its material to lay bare the moral disease that distorts it to its present shape.

The metaphor of vivisection is Joyce's own,[33] and it describes perfectly the art of such stories as "Two Gallants" or "Ivy Day in the Committee Room" or "Grace," an art swift, sharp, accurate, with every stroke deliberately measured. The tone is flat, grimly reticent; the style distant; the observation and metaphorical detail so consistently pointed that they achieve a kind of wit. Yet the success is not consistent. Some stories are too intent upon their analytical purposes. The formal neatness of "Eveline," "After the Race," "The Boarding House," and "Counterparts," for instance, is so obvious and oversimplifying, that the art comes to seem almost programmatic. These stories lack the vital detail pressing *against* the author's scalpel, and they also lack the author's rather malicious enjoyment both of his material and of his skill in dealing with it, which enliven "Two Gallants," "Ivy Day," "Grace," or even "A Little Cloud," "Clay," and "A Mother." But then, as all these images of spiritual decay succeed each other, we may well begin to question the mood of the book generally. Is not its tone, indeed its whole attitude to life, perhaps too insistently, and too constrictingly, "vivisective"?

Our answer inevitably reflects our view of Joyce's work as a whole. To some critics, *Dubliners* is a dispassionate, morally realistic account of modern life, Joyce's discovery of his lifelong attitude (ironical exposure) to his lifelong subject ("paralysis" and alienation). To others, his irony is "romantic," built upon the contrast between the individual's desires or feelings and the sordid realities of the modern world. To others again, his irony is only a device (like Chekhov's) for heightening the pity and terror of life.[34] Clearly, there are grounds for each of these judgments; but we also have to remember Joyce's relative immaturity when he wrote *Dubliners* and not be surprised if the book betrays it. Even while recognising the artistic success, we must also appreciate its limitations—not least because both help to explain Joyce's further development. And, not unnaturally, the limitations are very much those revealed more blatantly in *Stephen Hero*: an uncertain grasp of the values by which others are criticised, a vagueness about the genuine "life" by which simony and paralysis are constantly measured, a tendency to oversimplify reality in the process of exposing it.

It is not that the stories fail to imply the importance of courage, self-knowledge, fulfilment, freedom, or even the plainer domestic virtues; nor do they lack pity of a kind. But the comparison with Chekhov (or *Ulysses* for that matter) shows how little these values mean in *Dubliners*, how little it reveals what they might *be* in the actual experience of ordinary people, how complacent is its superior viewpoint. Some of the stories do reach towards a more self-critical, more specific, and hence (to that degree) deeper insight: "Araby," for example, "The Boarding House," "A Painful Case," and (most notably) "The Dead"—each, incidentally, the last in its respective group (childhood, adolescence, maturity, and public life).[35] But "Araby," for all its tone of mature wisdom, remains slightly evasive about how compromised the boy's romanticism really is; "The Boarding House" can only gesture vaguely towards the interconnexions between the mother's "simoniacal" plotting and the possibilities of life opening before her daughter as a result, symbolically suggesting only enough to make us realise how little the art realises (here and elsewhere) of the complicating paradoxes of life.

"A Painful Case" takes a rather longer step towards maturity. The stories immediately preceding it reveal an obvious pity for the frustrated lives they portray, but as Joyce's imagination is devoted less to the individual character than to the kind of situation he represents, so the pity is somewhat aloof, superior to its human object. "A Painful Case" deals with a related but deeper emotion: compassion. As many have pointed out, it portrays what Joyce felt he himself might have been (the central character, Mr Duffy, is actually modelled on Stanislaus);[36] it is also like a self-comment on the tone of much of *Dubliners*. For Mr Duffy is locked, irretrievably, in the Hell of his egocentric superiority to life. He refuses ordinary conventions and even ordinary carnal love; he disdains "to live, to err, to fall," and therefore, despite his literary pretensions, can never "triumph, . . . recreate life out of life."[37] Only the shock of Mrs Sinico's destruction enables him to see anything of his "paralysis," and then only partially and too late. The ending of the story illustrates perfectly what Joyce's art could achieve at this stage and what it could not. The recumbent figures in the park, where Mr Duffy stands at night, are still merely "venal and furtive loves" for him, though he despairs at his own loveless state. The subtle identification of the man and the "obstinate" and "laborious" engine disappearing into the darkness, his lapsing sense of reality, the perfectly silent darkness in which he feels himself alone, are precisely right. Nevertheless, the repeated phrase—"outcast from life's feast"—remains, as it must in the very terms in which the situation is observed, only the merest "symbol" of a life fuller and richer than his "rectitude" or the "venal and furtive loves."[38] The story gives it no more positive meaning than that. And what applies to "eating" here applies to a great many other "symbols" earnestly explicated by Joyce's critics; they are all *too* "suggestive" and therefore vague, too undefined dramatically. We could say that by choosing to work through the limited consciousness of his characters, Joyce found the best way to make their limitations imaginatively real, and thus avoided the need to define *his* position, to give meaning to his own stance in or behind the narrative, except by oblique "symbols" of the relevant values. We could equally well say that while he had no fuller sense of those values than he shows here, he simply could not see more in his characters than their limitations. The strength of *Dubliners* is the formal clarity, the subtlety and precision of its art—qualities that derive partly from a finely-sustained discipline but partly also from an immaturity of insight that made the formal problems relatively simple. Perhaps the most striking thing about the book, indeed, is the way Joyce turned his very limitations to account.

"The Dead," the last of the stories and the last written, is, I believe, the exception that proves the rule. It has been universally admired, and it is a minor masterpiece in its own right.[39] One important difference from the other stories is its protagonist. Gabriel Conroy is an intelligent and complex man, and Joyce's art is now at last capable of portraying him as such. In many ways he, too, represents a self Joyce might have been: a university teacher, a "man of letters" in a minor way, critical of Irish provincialism, sensitive to its frustrations—" 'O, to tell the truth, . . . I'm sick of my own country, sick of it!' "[40] That sickness is diagnosed very subtly, and a

D

second important difference from the other stories is the kind of irony that emerges. For there are no simple black-and-white judgments here, but rather a delicate balancing of insights. In fact, that balance is the story's central theme, and it heralds the spirit of Joyce's major works.

Gabriel's "sickness" is partly that he aspires to the wider and more vital possibilities he sees in Europe; partly that his education makes him feel morally superior to others; partly that he is unable to imagine others' lives sympathetically, so that a touch of egocentricity mars all his personal relations and all his judgments. At his aunts' annual party he is a favoured and admired guest, but he shows himself awkward, slightly pompous, inclined to resent others and to impose on them his own attitudes and his own good opinion of himself. Yet beneath all this lies an uncertainty, a genuine goodwill, and at bottom a saving humility. During the party a number of little frustrations jar his self-esteem. His impulse is to retreat: out of the tangled involvements of life to the clean, abstract, simple, and solitary world of the snow outside.[41] Significantly, we are made to perceive the bracing vigour which attracts him from the room, with its decaying echoes of once-vital social customs, as well as his evasion of the actual life the room contains. He is revealed as the victim of his self-ignorance. Ironically, the drunkard he despises proves capable of a spontaneous grace he could never manage;[42] he misses the ironical application to himself of his story about the old horse who could not break the habit of the treadmill;[43] ironically, he cannot appreciate his own speech toasting his aunts. To him they are "only two ignorant old women"[44]—like the old horse. What he says out of a mean and self-protective impulse expresses, beneath its sentimentality, a deeper truth than he realises: that traditions do live on and yet die, that life is choked and haunted by the dead and yet goes on. "We have all of us living duties and living affections which claim, and rightly claim, our strenuous endeavours. Therefore, I will not linger on the past. . . ."[45] The vividly evoked scene, the tangled relationships, the dramatically controlled symbolism, are created by a style now so responsive that it seems to disappear into the drama itself.

When Gabriel sees his wife on the stairs listening to an old ballad he asks himself what she is a symbol of. "*Distant Music* he would call the picture if he were a painter."[46] And being the man he is, he takes the music and its strange effect on her for his own. Suddenly he desires her, impatiently, thinking of their long intimacy together, alone, living in the "cold" with their mutual flame: "Like distant music these words that he had written years before were borne towards him from the past. He longed to be alone with her."[47] In truth, "he longed to be master of her strange mood."[48] The last shattering blow to his complacency is the truth about her mood—that it is not for him but the memory of a young man she had known years before, who had sung that ballad and who had died, in the brightness of his passionate love, for her. Gabriel is not insensitive; he sees his own egotism; but the "shameful consciousness of his own person" that now floods over him is not (as it is sometimes taken to be) the climactic moment of insight. It is only the reverse side of his egotism. He is no more merely a "ludicrous figure," a "nervous, well-meaning sentimentalist . . . idealizing his own clownish lusts," a "pitiable fatuous fellow," than his fellow-Dubliners are merely ignorant and foolish, drunkards, moral paralytics, mere gibbering ghosts of the past. One of the dramatic triumphs of the story is that we realize already what Gabriel must come to realise, know already what his listening wife was a symbol of. For a moment Gabriel nearly fails, and the moment, though dramatically unstressed, is a crucial act of self-criticism on Joyce's part:

'I think he died for me,' she answered.

A vague terror seized Gabriel at this answer, as if, at that hour when he had hoped to triumph, some impalpable and vindictive being was coming against him, gathering forces against him in its vague world. But he shook himself free of it with an effort of reason and continued to caress her hand. . . .[49]

The sense of some *external* evil, some "maleficent and sinful being," threatening the inviolate self—the assumption that dominates and limits the stories from the very first page—is here at last purged. Reason and love, an unspectacular but visibly "unresentful" and "generous" love, replace it; the veiled kinetic "riot" of self-defensive emotion gives way to a real *stasis* of spirit. And only now is Gabriel free, able to feel what the whole story has enacted: the complex tangle of distance and presence, passion and decay, love and detachment, aspiration and limit, life and death, in every individual and every society. The snow no longer represents to him the purity of the withdrawn self; as he "swoons" into unconsciousness, it seems to fall "like the descent of their last end, upon all the living and the dead."[50]

This story has often been compared with *Exiles* because of the personal and marital issues treated in both.[51] In more fundamental ways, however, it is prophetic of the end of *Ulysses*, where Leopold Bloom reaches at last a similar moral *stasis*; and perhaps also prophetic—in its rather equivocal "swooning" into the snow-world, a vast, undifferentiating state beyond all life and death— of *Finnegans Wake* as well. The swelling release of emotion is here just kept in control; with Molly Bloom and in *Finnegans Wake* it disguises itself more elaborately and escapes. But "The Dead" is finally unshaken. Its deeply felt conviction, its originality, the range and subtlety of its drama, its complex yet assured ironies, its humility before life, place it apart from the rest of *Dubliners*. Fine as they are, the other stories stand judged by this. In the six or seven years from the early poems, Joyce virtually found himself as a writer.

REFERENCES

1. *S.H.*, pp. 32–3, 37 (27–8, 33).
2. *Op. cit.*, p. 41 (37).
3. *Op. cit.*, p. 83 (78).
4. *Op. cit.*, pp. 231–2 (226); *M.B.K.*, pp. 166–8. For examples of this early verse, see E., pp. 83 ff.
5. *S.H.*, p. 179 (174).
6. *C.M.*, pp. 22 ff.
7. *Op. cit.*, esp. pp. 90 ff. Cp. J. R. Baker, "Joyce's *Chamber Music*," in *Arizona Quarterly*, xv (1959), pp. 349 ff. (On the order of the poems, cp. E., p. 272; *M.B.K.*, p. 225.)
8. H. Kenner, *Dublin's Joyce*, London 1955, pp. 39–42.
9. Cp. *C.M.*, pp. 95–6.
10. Cp. Ch. 3 below.
11. E., p. 603.
12. *M.B.K.*, p. 218; *L.*, p. 362.
13. *P.*, p. 219 (252).
14. E., pp. 153, 197.
15. Cp. Theodore Spencer's intro. to the 1944 edn. of *S.H.*, pp. 7–13; T. E. Connolly, "*Stephen Hero* Revisited," in *J.J.R.*, III (1959), pp. 40 ff.
16. H. Levin, *James Joyce, A Critical Introduction*, revised edn. London 1960, p. 52.
17. Cp. J. Prescott, "James Joyce's *Stephen Hero*," in *Journal of English and Germanic Philology*, LIII (1954), pp. 216 ff.
18. *S.H.*, pp. 150–1 (146–7).
19. Cp. *M.B.K.*, pp. 118, 170.
20. *S.H.*, p. 209 (204).
21. *Op. cit.*, p. 189 (184).
22. *Op. cit.*, p. 164 (159).
23. *Op. cit.*, p. 78 (74).
24. *Op. cit.*, pp. 72–3 (67–8).
25. *Op. cit.*, p. 198 (193).
26. *E.g.*, *op. cit.*, p. 199 (194).
27. *Op. cit.*, pp. 222–4 (217–18).
28. *Op. cit.*, pp. 223–4 (218).
29. *Op. cit.*, p. 207 (202).
30. M. Magalaner and R. M. Kain, *Joyce: the Man, the Work, the Reputation*, New York 1956, pp. 58 ff.; Allen Tate, "Three Commentaries," in *Sewanee Review*, LVIII (1950), p. 1. But cp. E., p. 171n.
31. See Magalaner and Kain, *Joyce*, pp. 68 ff. Other "symbolic" explications may be found in B. Ghiselin, "The Unity of James Joyce's *Dubliners*," in *Accent*, XVI (1956), pp. 75 ff., 196 ff.; M. Magalaner, *Time of Apprenticeship: The Fiction of the Young James Joyce*, New York and London 1959, ch. 3; W. Y. Tindall, *A*

Reader's Guide to James Joyce, New York 1959, ch. 1; but as criticisms of *literature* most of these strike me as either irrelevant or unconvincing.

32. Cp. A. Ostroff, "The Moral Vision in *Dubliners*," in *Western Speech*, xx (1956), pp. 196 ff.

33. *S.H.*, p. 190 (186).

34. *E.g.* Kenner, *Dublin's Joyce*, ch. 5; Levin, *James Joyce*, p. 41; Magalaner and Kain, *Joyce*, p. 62.

35. E., p. 216.

36. *M.B.K.*, p. 165; cp. E., p. 39.

37. *P.*, p. 176 (200).

38. *D.*, pp. 130–1 (146).

39. Cp. David Daiches, *The Novel and the Modern World*, rev. edn. Chicago and Cambridge 1960, pp. 73 ff.; Tate in *Sewanee Review* (1950); E., pp. 252 ff.; Ghiselin, in *Accent* (1956), pp. 207–11; Kenner, *Dublin's Joyce*, pp. 62–8; Magalaner and Kain, *Joyce* pp. 92–8 (though the last two seem to me to distort various aspects of the story).

40. *D.*, p. 216 (243).

41. *Op. cit.*, pp. 218–19 (246), 230 (259–60).

42. *Op. cit.*, p. 220 (248).

43. *Op. cit.*, p. 238 (267–8).

44. *Op. cit.*, p. 219 (247).

45. *Op. cit.*, p. 233 (262).

46. *Op. cit.*, p. 240 (270).

47. *Op. cit.*, p. 245 (275).

48. *Op. cit.*, p. 248 (279).

49. *Op. cit.*, p. 252 (283).

50. *Op. cit.*, p. 256 (288).

51. *E.g.* Levin, *James Joyce*, p. 43; Kenner, *Dublin's Joyce*, pp. 68–9.

CHAPTER III

PORTALS OF DISCOVERY:
A PORTRAIT OF THE ARTIST AS A YOUNG MAN AND *EXILES*

With *A Portrait of the Artist as a Young Man* Joyce did find himself—in both senses of the phrase. In re-creating the process by which he had become his present self, he also confirmed the artistic maturity to which, as he saw it looking back, that process had been reaching, obscurely but continually. The result is a work far more "difficult" than any he had written before, but also so much finer and more complex (and so often misunderstood) that it calls for a correspondingly more detailed examination.

The first thing Joyce discovered in this backward vision was a pattern of moral growth and social alienation —a pattern typical of European society at least since the Romantics.[1] The individual grows to consciousness within a specific social environment and is partly moulded by its pressures; but as he grows, he increasingly finds his society too fragmented, too materialistic, and too restrictive to sustain him. It offers him neither spiritual nourishment nor a usable culture, yet it is too powerful to be resisted or easily changed. If the individual is an artist his problem is especially acute. Just because of his greater sensitivity, he is forced apart from his society; just because of his alienation, he comes to represent its general condition in the clearest possible form. His position is riddled with the familiar paradoxes of much nineteenth- and twentieth-century art: he is at once a member of his society, a rebel, a martyr, and the possible saviour in whose imagination "the spirit of man makes a continual affirmation."[2]

For all its verve and clarity, *Stephen Hero* could portray nothing of all that. With brilliant economy, Joyce now selected from his life everything that could. He developed, foreshortened, and remoulded the past; related and ordered his experience in the light of his fuller understanding; until at last he made the experience of Stephen ("protomartyr") Dedalus ("fabulous artificer") show how, "for the millionth time," in the specific circumstances of late nineteenth-century Dublin, the conscience of the race was forged in the smithy of a human soul.[3] Instead of fictionalised autobiography, he now created an autobiographical drama.

This involved more than rendering Stephen's life and his society without the crude authorial interference of the earlier version. As his conception of the book deepened so his artistic problems became more difficult. Stephen's consciousness was both the stage and the protagonist of the drama, and its growth was the action. But that growth was not, as Joyce saw it, simply the process of Stephen's deepening alienation from his society.[4] It was also a positive process of understanding, both of the society he saw about him and of the emotions he felt within himself as he lived in that society—though an understanding always imperfect, always limited by the limitations of his youth. Joyce had to convey the successive stages of Stephen's awareness of life; or, what was ultimately the same thing, he had to portray the nature of Stephen's world as he actually experienced it. Furthermore, he had to show how Stephen's experience gradually enabled him to distinguish between himself and his environment, to grasp more accurately what each was and how they were really interrelated. To make this complex process vivid and dramatically convincing was the first problem.

Part of the answer was to portray the world in terms of Stephen's direct awareness of it. Catching the texture, the flow of what Stephen sees and feels at crucial points in his development would not only reveal the nature of his environment but would define Stephen's self at the same time. Thus the *how* of Stephen's experience was as important as the *what*: indeed, the two had to be shown as the same thing. But the underlying contours of Stephen's consciousness—his basic character—had also to be felt within the flow of his experience. Similarly, his limitations, his mistakes, his distortions of vision at each particular stage had to be made imaginatively real as well. Style and symbol and structure had all to be used with an intense dramatic purposefulness, so that together they would become the medium, the very substance, in which the drama could be made visible and precise. The mature technical skill with which Joyce saw—and solved—his problems in the *Portrait* is a large part of his achievement. Not only is the book extraordinarily sharp and objective for an autobiographical novel (a form notoriously difficult); it is, in fact, one of the most tightly economical novels ever written.

What gives this technical achievement its point, however, is the dramatic *understanding* of which it is the medium, a moral maturity correspondingly subtle and pervasive. At bottom, all of Joyce's technical problems arose from the need to understand himself, in the widest sense of the term. He had to comprehend not only what, as a younger man, he had felt only obscurely and seen only partially, but he had also to understand his earlier limitations. He had to follow the *kinesis* of the young man's life until it was fulfilled in true, objective contemplation—*stasis*. In other words, his basic problem was to achieve the genuine freedom, the sympathetic but detached insight necessary to the "dramatic" artist, and to do so with a subject—the early evolution of the dramatic artist himself—where the difficulties were especially acute. The title of the book suggests the balance he sought. It is a self-portrait, but of a self now partly outgrown, yet also, in the writing of the book, now partly fulfilled. To reach that insight meant perceiving the social malaise exemplified in his own life, but it also meant discriminating the lines of genuine growth even within his earlier confusions. To write the *Portrait* was to discover how and why his mistakes were really "volitional" and really "portals of discovery."

The temptations he faced were partly those of any autobiographer, partly those of a man deeply critical of his society. It would have been easy to slip again into emotional identification with Stephen Hero, and to treat him simply as a sensitive, artistic, lonely and heroic soul who gradually rises superior to his environment and takes off to "freedom" and "art" on the wings of his ethereal ideals. On the other hand, it would have been just as easy, and just as false, to go to the opposite extreme. It would have been quite possible simply to reject Stephen as a *persona* he had now sloughed off completely, and to dismiss him, with his sentimental idealism and bitterness, his moral instability, his acrid frustrations, as a figure with whom "there is no question whatever of his regeneration," and who is doomed only to Romantic *hybris* and collapse.[5] Joyce fell into neither trap; and if his readers have seen only one or the other of these judgments in the book, the reason is that Joyce holds both of them in the balance of his larger comprehension.

Stephen himself, like the early Joyce, oscillates between moods of romantic idealism and bitter "irony," groping his way towards an "indifference" he slowly comes to see as his possible salvation. But only the author of the *Portrait*, in understanding the process, could achieve the relevant kind of "indifference," and writing the *Portrait* is the act in which he does so. His vision, his judgment have become truly objective; what he sees in looking back and what he feels about it are fused in the visible drama. And his "irony" becomes something other than the uncertain, self-protective device it had been. It has now a different character altogether. In the *Portrait* it becomes the mark of a sym-

pathetic patience, an imagination large enough to
embrace the tangles and paradoxes of life as they are
without rushing at once to reduce them to abstract sim-
plicities. Joyce's attitude to Stephen has been well
described as "amused, detached, sympathetic, simultaneously critical and non-judgmental";[6] this is the
poise of a mind now free at last to contemplate itself and
to re-create its own slow development to that very
freedom. The earlier *kinesis* has given way to a "dramatic"
impersonality, an impersonality that wears an ironic
smile, if only because it includes its own existence within
its understanding. For the *Portrait*, more than an autobiographical novel, or even a study of artistic alienation,
is that peculiar twentieth-century phenomenon: a work
of art which is at once a representative fable, a moral
history, and (through these) a kind of demonstration of
its own significance *as* a work of art.

Joyce's attitudes to Stephen and to Dublin are never
openly stated, of course. Rather, "the artist, like the God
of creation, remains within or behind or beyond or above
his handiwork, invisible, refined out of existence."[7] The
art is thoroughly dramatic in every sense. Joyce allows
its action to speak its own meaning in its own terms. His
attitudes inform the action, but they shape and order it
from within so that we see their justification in feeling the
logic with which the novel unfolds. He here achieves the
insight and the capacity on which his two finest works
were to be founded.

Right from the opening pages of the *Portrait*, in fact,
we are made to see the operative principle of Joyce's art
in the story itself. Stephen's childish "experience of life"
consists at first only of fragments. He comes to understand them only when, and to the extent that, he can
relate and order them, and in ordering he necessarily
evaluates. Real and imaginary objects, events, sensations,
words, desires, fears, prohibitions, threats, puzzling and
terrible scenes, associations, all cohere for the child in

more and more complex patterns. And as they do so his grasp of language grows more secure.[8] For it is in more and more complex patterns of language—in the ambiguous meanings of "sick," for example,[9] or "politics,"[10] or phrases like "Tower of Ivory. House of Gold,"[11] or in poems,[12] or in a passage from Newman,[13] or even philosophical terms from Aquinas,[14]—that he expresses the external world as he understands it and at the same time expresses the very form of his understanding.

To master language is for Stephen, as it was for Joyce, only the outward aspect of a deeper effort. He has to strike a balance between his inner life of desires, hopes and fears (the values that shape his aspirations and actions), and the outer life of cold and warmth, threats and praise, political and religious pressures (the hard facts that resist him and force him constantly to discipline his inner life and reform his values more objectively). He has to balance a necessary engagement with the outer world and a necessary separation from it. Only by doing so can he orientate himself—or rather, define his self—adequately in relation to it.[15] The puzzled, lonely, fearful little boy who is jostled by the external world at Clongowes Wood School, and who tries to write down his address in a universe too enormous for him even to imagine,[16] eventually becomes the young man who goes off to discover on his own "what the heart is and what it feels" in the still unplumbed immensities of "life."[17] But although the ignorance, the loneliness, and the fear still remain (like a rocky substratum), the young man is now conscious of them; and to the extent that he can now evaluate their importance and their unimportance, he is capable of controlling them. What he comes slowly (though only partly) to realise is that he must avoid both the cold, indifferent alienation from other people to which he can be so easily pushed by his very idealism and intelligence, and equally the heart-warming but ultimately corrupting effects of submission to the ruling

values of his society. His plight and his problem are
universal ones. And as he moves through one portal of
discovery to the next, he moves from more or less instinctive fantasies and actions, to acts of imagination and
of will more deliberate, more fully and humanly rational.

As Hugh Kenner has remarked, each of the five
chapters of the *Portrait* concentrates on one of Stephen's
major problems: "ego *vs* authority" in 1, 3, and 5, and
"Dublin *vs* the dream" in 2 and 4. Each chapter, he
observes, successively "gathers up the thematic material
of the preceding ones and entwines them with a dominant
theme of its own," closing with "a synthesis of triumph
which the next destroys."[18] But this indicates only one
side of the process. What is not so generally noticed is that
each chapter also portrays a positive achievement; in
each one, some basic potentiality of Stephen's life is
fulfilled. The theme of the book is *growth*. To misread
Joyce's judgments is to miss the fineness of his art.

The first two chapters, for example, measure the boy's
world as the boy begins to discover himself in it. With
delicate precision, Joyce catches the child's impulses, his
puzzling, even frightening, environment, and the gap
between the two. The boy's values gradually form in his
experience, in his fantasies as much as in what he sees and
suffers, and gradually lead him to apply them *to* his
experience. The first chapter gathers to a climax in his
appeal—almost instinctive—to the Rector of his school
for justice, and in the delusions of moral maturity after
his "victory." But Joyce does show us a real victory,
which the delusions limit but cannot destroy. Stephen's
action uncovers what we have seen his character and
experience slowly produce in him: a moral sense and a
moral courage basic to everything to come. The second
chapter traces out more complex impulses and fantasies
in him as external reality seems correspondingly more
complex and more grimy. He protects himself by silent
aloofness; he develops "romantic" yearnings. But again

Joyce's irony lies in the subtlety of his judgment. The aloofness, we see, does protect Stephen; he now can, and he does, resist the moral cheapness of his world; and his yearnings for beauty and love do represent a need that his environment cannot answer. It can only drive him into shame and guilt and deeper isolation and, finally, into the arms of a whore. Although he again suffers delusions of maturity as a result, the need and its satisfaction are none the less real for that. The sexual encounter, the now half-instinctive, half-deliberate act of surrender and discovery, is part of his growth. Given his social and moral circumstances, it exacerbates the divisions between his body and his soul, but it also discovers another undeniable part of himself and of the world he inhabits.

The same is true even in the third chapter, which lays bare the ugly spirit of Irish Catholicism as Stephen experiences it, and where we might expect Joyce to show the same savage hostility as in *Stephen Hero*. At first sight it seems as if he does. The divisions in Stephen between matter and spirit, between his lust and his correspondingly sentimental idealism, are reflected with grim fidelity in his religion. Crude, legalistic, authoritarian, based upon the subtle materialism of terror, the sermons on Hell are calculated to produce just such a reaction as Stephen's: a wild flight back to sexual horror and guilt. For once he does confess; his characteristic sensitivity to the mysteries of faith and ritual make him especially vulnerable to what his masters offer him as religion. The value of his crude religiosity, the natural response to what he is offered, is obvious in its very portrayal.[19] But the sermons contain more than grotesque horror, nightmares almost comic in their literal-mindedness. Stephen soon sloughs off the ethical clichés, the "hangman God" who hates and punishes the life of nature, the ecclesiastical bullying. On the other hand, some of the crucial terms will remain to enter the very substance of his life: the "one thing needful," for example; the image of

Satan uttering his "*non serviam*"; the image of the Re-
deemer calling men to a new Gospel; the pains of Hell
for those who will not submit; and above all the conception of his soul's vocation as a destiny at once necessary
and liberating, the one way to fulfil his nature and
achieve salvation, a task to which he must direct all
physical and moral effort and whose demands in turn
impose a shape upon his life.

Chapter 4 is his discovery of that vocation, and it is
here that he really confronts his religion. The chapter
repeats yet develops the now familiar pattern. Stephen
considers, then rejects the priesthood. Once again his
decision is instinctive, but now he quickly comes to
recognise the reasons for his instinct, and his subsequent
discovery that he wants to be an artist is an act of almost
fully conscious self-knowledge. And once again his discovery is limited by his mistake about its true nature, by
his still immature soul.

Clearly, he is attracted to the priesthood by very mixed
feelings—partly a genuine religious sense, partly isolation
from others. His temper is still "romantic." Able to feel
neither love nor hate, his mind left "lucid and indifferent" even in the midst of his fervent devotions, he is
inevitably drawn to an abstract, compensating "love" of
God. But now he is conscious of his temperamental
"indifference," and the self-knowledge he has so pain-
fully acquired helps him to further understanding.
Failing to "merge his life in the common tide of other
lives" even by devotion, he is made aware of his "spiritual
dryness," doubts, and scruples.[20] And imagining what the
priesthood would mean to him, he soon feels it chill.
Memories of his past, the knowledge he has gained of his
own physical and moral nature, now all coalesce in a
decisive impulse:

Some instinct, waking at these memories, stronger than
education or piety, quickened within him at every near

approach to that life [of the Jesuit College], an instinct subtle and hostile, and armed him against aquiescence. The chill and order of the life repelled him. . . . His destiny was to be elusive of social or religious orders. . . . The snares of the world were its ways of sin. He would fall. He had not yet fallen but he would fall silently, in an instant. . . .[21]

And so he discovers what he cannot be. He smiles when he thinks of the "disorder, the misrule and confusion of his father's house" which has won his allegiance.[22] He recognises in his brothers and sisters "the voice of Nature herself," with its "pain and weariness yet hope of better things."[23] He sees something of the truth about himself and about human life, but of course he does not see all. The image that comes to him of the solitary farmhand, "considering in turn the four points of the sky and then regretfully plunging his spade in the earth," bears a subtle application to himself, who must also eventually plunge his spade in the earth. His awareness of "Nature's children" is still only theoretical, filtered through a quotation from Newman. And the immaturity, the half-blindness, also affects his crucial discovery: "The end he had been born to serve yet did not see had led him to escape by an unseen path. . . . He had refused. Why?"[24]

To us, the answer was already apparent at the moment when Stephen had parted from the Jesuit Director. It lay in the difference between his smile at a song in the street and the "mirthless reflection of the sunken day" in the priest's face.[25] Now he comes to discover the answer himself. At first it seems only a love of language, a positive impulse towards "the poise and balance" (the phrase is more significant than he yet knows) to be created in words. Characteristically, he is also more attracted towards "the contemplation of an inner world of individual emotions mirrored perfectly in a lucid supple periodic prose," than to the verbal reflexion of "the glowing sensible world."[26] His ideals are unrelated to each other, but it is out of them both that the "poise and balance" of the *Portrait* itself are to grow.

For Stephen, however, there is at this stage a different revelation. He seems to hear "a voice from beyond the world" calling him to venture forth. In an ecstasy of excitement, he decides that he must and will:

His soul had arisen from the grave of boyhood, spurning her graveclothes. Yes! Yes! Yes! He would create proudly out of the freedom and power of his soul, as the great artificer whose name he bore, a living thing, new and soaring and beautiful, impalpable, imperishable.[27]

As Hugh Kenner has pointed out, all this rapture is accompanied by an ironic dramatic commentary.[28] The voices actually to be heard calling on the shore are those of Stephen's classmates—"Come along, Dedalus! Bous Stephanoumenos! Bous Stephaneforos!" "Duck him! Guzzle him now, Towser!"[29] As Stephen dreams of flying like his mythical namesake, "a hawk like man flying sunward above the sea," their shouts break in again: "One! Two!... Look out!" "Oh, Cripes, I'm drownded!"[30] These are the voices of the earth Stephen aspires to leave on the wings of imagination. They embody at once a jeer, a threat, and a warning. In their crudeness, they represent "the sluggish matter of the earth" that Stephen aspires to transform into beauty. But of course Stephen is too romantically impatient to accept and understand the sluggish earth; as yet he is unable to plunge his spade into it and cultivate his beauty from out of its apparent ugliness. His only reaction is to parry the jeer, and to ignore the ugliness, to seek only an obvious, romantic Beauty. His mood lifts into even more rapturously "lyrical" prose: "He was alone. He was unheeded, happy and near to the wild heart of life. He was alone and young and wilful and wildhearted," etc., etc.[31]

E

The birdlike girl he sees standing silent in the water lifts him still higher:

—Heavenly God! cried Stephen's soul, in an outburst of profane joy. . . . Her eyes had called to him and his soul had leaped at the call. To live, to err, to fall, to triumph, to recreate life out of life! . . . On and on and on and on![32]

There are significant echoes of earlier "triumphs," but once again there is knowledge discovered amid the delusions. To be an artist it is first necessary to realise that one wants to be an artist; and if this young man is still years distant from the mature writer, maturity after all comes from living through such groping, stumbling self-discoveries as this.

And so the last chapter, as we might expect, leads Stephen at last towards a rational, analytic, *critical* consciousness. He now examines his world, his vocation, and himself, until finally he becomes aware of what he must do: learn what "life" *is* by himself living it as he must, which seems to mean living it outside Ireland. His immaturity, however, does not drop from him with a miraculous, climactic thump of insight. Joyce is too faithful to the gradual processes of life for the clichés of "middlebrow" fiction. But neither is the chapter merely "a mournful diminuendo" of Stephen's guilt and anxiety and barren isolation.[33] Joyce is too faithful to the gradual processes of life for clichés of "highbrow" irony either. Although he has discovered his vocation, Stephen is still in the kinetic state he was before—on the one hand full of "loathing and bitterness" for the sordid world, on the other dreaming about "the essence of beauty" while the world "perishes about his feet."[34] We are shown him, in fact, adopting that superior, clinical "indifference" to the squalid city that lies behind Joyce's own early work, an "indifference" now seen for the self-protective evasion it really is. But even while he "vivisects" this "romantic temper," Joyce now shows his own growth beyond it by also perceiving the power of growth in Stephen. The young man's "romantic temper" is constantly placed against potentialities in him of a temper more stable, more integrated and fruitful, the seeds of the "classical temper" which eventually enabled the mature artist to make just these necessary criticisms of his earlier self.

This mature poise explains why at first sight Stephen appears so puzzling a mixture in this last chapter and so difficult to sum up. His understanding of Ireland, abstract and rather subjective as it is, is set beside his frightened recoil from her actual face.[35] His high pretensions as a "priest of the eternal imagination" are set beside the poem he actually writes, as "dewy wet" as his soul,[36] though it *is*, all the same, a poem of sorts and the worst we can say of it is that most of Joyce's were not much better. His "fear of the unknown" is set beside his courage to reject and venture, and beside the raucous conventionality and the cowardice of his fellow-students.[37] Joyce rather overdoes the dullness of Stephen's fellows: the bores become somewhat boring, the odd sympathiser somewhat wooden. For moments, here and there, the old identification of *Stephen Hero* threatens to return. But Joyce manages to hold the balance, partly because he can now make Stephen himself half-aware of the issues. His mind, as he is forced to admit, is "supersaturated" with the religion he rejects; he half-realises he is not positively, creatively free;[38] nevertheless, he also realises that in order to "hit the conscience" of his countrymen he must at least free himself negatively, from allegiances and influences that would corrupt:

I will not serve that in which I no longer believe, whether it call itself my home, my fatherland, or my church: and I will try to express myself in some mode of life or art as freely as I can and as wholly as I can, using for my defence the only arms I allow myself to use—silence, exile, and cunning.

. . . I do not fear to be alone or to be spurned for another or to leave whatever I have to leave. And I am not afraid to make a mistake, even a great mistake, a lifelong mistake, and perhaps as long as eternity too.[39]

His positive ambition marks the limits of his self-knowledge. It is vague, apparently only a callow, romantic, irresponsible self-glorification. His alienation from his society leaves him alone and apparently rootless, cut off from everything that constitutes "life." And yet his rejections have a moral edge which we have seen ground by the whole of the preceding action, and his self-dedication to "life or art" is so concentrated, so complete, that his only formula for it is obviously inadequate to what he means.

His aesthetic theory reveals what he now possesses and what he does not. His ideas are perceptive, ordered, yet only ideas and only partly valid ideas at that. At times they are expounded with a slightly alarming pomposity. While he knows that his vocation entails a discipline, he does not know how deep that discipline has to be. To define "beauty" in purely formal terms, to reject the demands a philistine society makes of a writer, to insist on the artist's integrity to his art—all this is within his capacity. But to understand that moral choices are not purely "kinetic" reactions of the nerves, that art is rooted in the moral and social life of mankind and that the artist has responsibilities to this—responsibilities which are the true motive for resisting the philistines, that the objectivity and "indifference" of the dramatic artist has nothing of cold, withdrawn superiority to life about it but is rather a wisdom wrung from the process of living—all this is just beyond his present grasp. His conception of "the literary tradition" is now seen as part of his immaturity.[40] His desire to extricate an ideal beauty away from the brute reality of the world,[41] like his rigid dichotomy between the "animal" and the "mental" world,[42] is clearly a symptom of the same thing. As he expounds his theory, the "sluggish," "harsh" setting seems to him only "to war against the course of [his] thought";[43] his admiring friend, Lynch, betrays not only the bitter frustrations underlying his own approval,[44] but also the motives and the weakness of Stephen's position: "What do you mean," he asks at the end, ". . . by prating about beauty and the imagination in this miserable Godforsaken island?"[45] The question goes deeper than either of them realises. But there is another side. Stephen's theory (like Joyce's early ideas) also reveals an impressive ability to learn for himself what nothing in his environment could teach him. And among the things he is beginning to learn are the need for "patience"[46] and for experience. As he says, "when we come to the phenomena of artistic conception, artistic gestation and artistic reproduction I require a new terminology and a new personal experience."[47]

At last he is beginning to turn his critical intelligence upon himself. To some readers he may seem in the end only an "indigestibly Byronic" aesthete, totally lacking in humour, a mere "victim being prepared for sacrifice" on the altar of Joyce's ironical criticism in *Ulysses*.[48] Even at his worst, however, he is never quite as hopeless as that (nor Joyce's irony quite so simple); but it is just of the end of the book that it is least true. By turning to Stephen's diary, the end reveals, more vividly perhaps than in any other way, the first signs of humour in him, directed upon his own heroics, his own attitudes, his own "vague words for a vague emotion."[49] What is more, there are signs of a new humility: the beginnings of wisdom. Although he still cannot integrate what he feels and what he sees, he can now begin to appreciate (and exploit) the gap between them for himself:

[voices] call to me, their kinsman, making ready to go, shaking the wings of their exultant and terrible youth.

April 26. Mother is putting my new secondhand clothes in order. She prays now, she says, that I may learn in my own life and away from home and friends what the heart is and what it feels. Amen. So be it. Welcome, O life! I go to encounter for the millionth time the reality of experience and to forge in the smithy of my soul the uncreated conscience of my race. . . .[50]

Stephen's immaturity and his achieved growth measure and qualify each other. He calls upon his mythical namesake, Daedalus, "old father, old artificer," as he prepares for flight. For himself, he seems to take the ambiguous role of Icarus, who flew too high and drowned, the fearful son seeking the mature father. The father he calls upon is the artist who seeks his "son" (who seeks, that is, his own created self-image), and who is now, in the *Portrait*, mature enough to find him—in this immature Stephen. The same balanced, ironic insight is sustained to the end.

In that, of course, lies the source of the novel's achievement: its integrity, the clarity and firmness of its vision, the maturity that is expressed in, and gives imaginative life to, the subtly controlled, subtly textured prose. What was self-discovery for Joyce, a personal achievement, is made into an impersonal one—a "dramatic" work of art in which we can behold the image of a universal truth. But equally, of course, we have to recognise how much its strength also rests upon its strictly limited scope. Everything is concentrated upon Stephen. It is his growth on which every detail, every incident, every character, every movement of the action is focused. That growth, as we have seen, reveals a good deal about his world at large: his weaknesses are its weaknesses as well. But naturally, in showing this so brilliantly, the novel cannot reveal more of life than Stephen's very limited consciousness can engage with or than is implied by his weaknesses. And looking back, we see that one condition of Joyce's success in the *Portrait* is the same as in *Dubliners*: by concentrating on Stephen's actual experience of the world, he could make his growth a vividly immediate drama, but at the same time he could only portray what in that world had to be outgrown or rejected in the process of growth. If the *Portrait* lacks the rich, broadly-ranging, comic vitality of *Ulysses*, or even the amused observation of some of *Dubliners*, it is not because Joyce temporarily lost his native liveliness. It is simply that, in the very terms of his novel, he could not show what "life" did come to mean to the young man. He could not dramatise more of the deeper vision to which Stephen is groping than is embodied in the portrayal of his groping itself. Hence the need for a sequel, *Ulysses*.

The world and the issues of the *Portrait* are thus limited to what Joyce himself at that time could hold firmly in his grasp—a personal experience now at last comprehended and "placed." A comparison with his play, *Exiles* (written immediately after the *Portrait*), is instructive. Here he ventured for the first time into other issues, through further portals of discovery; but probably no one else has thought as highly of the result as Joyce did.

The themes proposed in the play were obviously close to Joyce himself in 1914. The spiritual integrity of the artist (Richard Rowan), now returning to Ireland from voluntary exile, is played against the life of desire and impulse, against the compromise with conventional values, typical of the ordinary man of talent who has stayed at home (Robert Hand). Within Richard himself, the spirit of his mother's cold, hard, in-turned righteousness plays against the spirit of his generous, smiling, handsome father. It is a conflict in him between ego-centric bitterness and generosity of spirit. The main "situation," however—Bertha Rowan's possible infidelity with Robert Hand—opens up rather different questions about the nature of love. To Robert, it is simply desire, passion, ultimately the *possession* of a physical pleasure. To Bertha, it is a complete loyalty, the attachment of one's affective life to another person, ultimately a kind of *giving* of one's self. To Richard, it is more than it is to Robert and less than it is to Bertha: a union both physical and spiritual, but a union which depends upon a completely free choice and therefore upon the complete moral independence, the ultimate isolation, of the individuals concerned. As he watches (and half-engineers) Robert's attempted seduction of his wife, his "spiritual" values fight against Robert's "materialism," his insistence on personal freedom against Bertha's moral dependence on him. He struggles to *use* his jealousy in order to place their union "in the region of the difficult, the void and the impossible", as Joyce's working-notes phrase it:[51] only if the union could be broken can its continuance have meaning.

Thus the nature of freedom becomes the central issue of the play. On the one hand, Robert speaks the heroic, Superman language of Richard's youth: "All life is a conquest, the victory of human passion over the commandments of cowardice";[52] "there is no law before impulse."[53] Richard, on the other hand, now speaks a different, maturer language. All he will recommend to others is, "Free yourself."[54] For him, freedom now appears to lie not simply in personal impulse, nor in mere rejection of conventional values. It is rather an existential choice, an act of the whole being made in the knowledge that each individual is finally alone in the void, responsible only to his own conscience, but nevertheless fully responsible to that. Thus he feels guilty lest he distort Bertha's moral life by limiting her power of choice.[55] Believing that the individual must, and can, stand utterly alone in order to choose, he does his best to force Robert and Bertha into freedom, though neither of them seems to understand or want or even feel capable of it.

They want to give themselves to a moral centre outside themselves; he must refuse to accept their allegiance, their "love." He knows (as Joyce's notes point out)[56] that Bertha is not Robert's mistress but he imagines she might be: only in this way can he achieve an existential freedom for himself even if he fails to lead the others to it:

RICHARD [. . . *taking her head between his hands, bends it back and gazes long into her eyes.*] I have a deep, deep wound of doubt in my soul. . . .
[*Still gazing at her and speaking as if to an absent person.*] I have wounded my soul for you—a deep wound of doubt which can never be healed. I can never know, never in this world. I do not wish to know or to believe. I do not care. It is not in the darkness of belief that I desire you. But in restless living wounding doubt. To hold you by no bonds, even of love, to be united with you in body and soul in utter nakedness—for this I longed. And now I am tired for a while, Bertha. My wound tires me.[57]

This passage from the ending of the play, however, illustrates the central weakness of the whole work: the sentimentality with which its hero seems imbued, a sentimentality so obvious that some critics have supposed Joyce *meant* it as an "ironical" repudiation of Richard's position.[58] Perhaps *Exiles* would have been better if he had; nevertheless, it would not be the play Joyce evidently thought it was. He does, it is true, treat Richard with a certain amount of irony (his masochism, for instance, or his unconscious wish to be betrayed), but never to the point of repudiation. The trouble is rather that the irony here, unlike that of the *Portrait*, is never properly focused because the things to which it is applied —especially Richard—are themselves never properly focused. Too many of the crucial facts and issues and values remain (again unlike the *Portrait*) rather factitious, *un*dramatised, and we have to fill in the blanks ourselves.

It is as if Joyce were standing too near his subject. We never feel the objective, living reality of the "man" Richard's wife is supposed to have made of him; and because we don't, we cannot really understand certain things we should. We cannot tell, for example, how much his "integrity" is merely the legacy of his mother's emotional impotence. His allegedly impressive art seems only to express his "scorn" and "bitterness" and "loneliness"; what else it might contain remains a mystery. We do not know if his "delicate, strange, and highly sensitive conscience," as Joyce describes it,[59] has ever worked on behalf of another person. For all his talk about "love" and "union," what we see is egocentric wilfulness and isolation. And his final declaration (with its dubious mixture of self-pity and self-congratulation) seems completely to forget the necessary bonds of our human flesh, the attachments and values we do not wholly choose but which (as in the *Portrait*) grow in us by the very process of living in a given environment. But since we cannot accept Robert's sort of claims for the material world in which we must live, and yet the claims he (or Bertha) ought to make are not made, Richard remains dramatically "unplaced." What does the silence on Joyce's part mean? Not, I think, that he remained beyond his handiwork, allowing the action itself to expose Richard's barrenness[60] (for Richard's beliefs are not, and hardly seem intended as, *necessarily* barren). Nor is it even that the naturalistic, Ibsenesque conventions of his play hindered him from being clear.[61] It is rather that he failed, as he had failed in other works, fully to comprehend his experience so that he could dramatise it, could project it with such concreteness and objectivity that its meaning would emerge from within as an impersonal truth. We hardly need to consult Ellmann's biography[62] to learn how much of Joyce's own marital life went into the play; unfortunately, the disturbance reveals itself. If Richard Rowan is an ambiguous hero, it does not mean that Joyce succeeded in being "ironical"; it only means that *Exiles*, like the *Portrait*, but for very different reasons, was also a preparation for *Ulysses*. Indeed, as *Stephen Hero* is to the *Portrait*, so *Exiles* is to *Ulysses*: the uncertain ironies, the issues imperfectly grasped, and therefore imperfectly dramatised, in the one are transformed in the maturer and richer drama of the other.

REFERENCES

1. On art and society in the *P.*, cp. James T. Farrell, *The League of Frightened Philistines*, London 1948, pp. 35 ff.; J. H. Jack, "Art and *The Portrait of the Artist*," in *Essays in Criticism*, v (1955), pp. 354 ff.; M. Beebe, "Joyce and Stephen Dedalus," in *J.J.M.S.*, pp. 67 ff.

2. *S.H.*, p. 85 (80).

3. *P.*, p. 257 (299).

4. But cp. Kenner, *Dublin's Joyce*, ch. 8; and M. Schorer, "Technique as Discovery," in *Forms of Modern Fiction*, ed. W. Van O'Connor, Minneapolis 1948, pp. 9 ff.

5. Kenner, *Dublin's Joyce*, p. 112.

6. S. H. Poss, "A Portrait of the Artist as Beginner," in *University of Kansas City Review*, xxvi (1960), p. 192.

7. *P.*, p. 219 (252).

8. Cp. Levin, *James Joyce*, pp. 53–4; Dorothy Van Ghent, *The English Novel, Form and Function*, New York 1953, pp. 265 ff.

9. *P.*, p. 13 (9).

10. *Op. cit.*, p. 17 (13).

11. *Op. cit.*, p. 44 (45).

12. *Op. cit.*, pp. 24 (22), 99 (108), 227–8 (262–3).

13. *Op. cit.*, pp. 168 (190), 169 (192).

14. *Op. cit.*, pp. 190 ff. (216 ff.).

15. Cp. Van Ghent, *The English Novel*, esp. p. 275.

16. *P.*, pp. 15–16 (11–12).

17. *Op. cit.*, p. 257 (299).

18. Kenner, *Dublin's Joyce*, pp. 123, 125, 129.

19. *P.*, pp. 149 (168), 151 (171).

20. *Op. cit.*, pp. 153–5 (173–5).

21. *Op. cit.*, pp. 164–5 (187–8).

22. *Op. cit.*, pp. 165–7 (188–9).

23. *Op. cit.*, p. 168 (190).

24. *Op. cit.*, pp. 169–70 (191–2).

25. *Op. cit.*, p. 163 (186).

26. *Op. cit.*, p. 171 (193).

27. *Op. cit.*, p. 174 (197).

28. Cp. Kenner, *Dublin's Joyce*, pp. 99, 131–2.

29. *P.*, p. 172 (195).

30. *Op. cit.*, p. 173 (197).

31. *Op. cit.*, p. 175 (199).

32. *Op. cit.*, p. 176 (200).

33. W. Y. Tindall, *James Joyce, His Way of Interpreting the Modern World*, New York and London 1950, p. 21.

34. *P.*, pp. 179–80 (205).
35. *Op. cit.*, pp. 186–7 (213–14).
36. *Op. cit.*, pp. 221 ff. (254 ff.).
37. *Op. cit.*, pp. 230 ff. (265 ff.) 239 ff. (276 ff.), 246 (285), 251–2 (292).
38. *Op. cit.*, pp. 242 ff. (281 ff.).
39. *Op. cit.*, p. 251 (291).
40. *Op. cit.*, p. 192 (219).
41. *Op. cit.*, p. 193 (221).
42. *Op. cit.*, p. 210 (241).
43. *Op. cit.*, pp. 211 (242), 213 (245).
44. *Op. cit.*, p. 216 (248).
45. *Op. cit.*, p. 219 (252).
46. *Op. cit.*, p. 198 (226).
47. *Op. cit.*, p. 214 (245–6).
48. Kenner, *Dublin's Joyce*, p. 132.
49. *P.*, p. 255 (297).
50. *Op. cit.*, p. 257 (299).
51. *Exiles*, p. 164 (114).
52. *Op. cit.*, p. 99 (71).
53. *Op. cit.*, p. 125 (87).
54. *Op. cit.*, p. 100 (71).
55. *Op. cit.*, pp. 93–4 (67), 96 (68).
56. *Op. cit.*, p. 172 (123).
57. *Op. cit.*, p. 162 (112).
58. *E.g.* Kenner, *Dublin's Joyce* ch. 6.
59. *Exiles*, p. 165 (116).
60. *E.g.* Francis Fergusson, *The Human Image in Dramatic, Literature*, New York 1957, pp. 72 ff.
61. Cp. Levin, *James Joyce*, p. 44; R. Williams, "The *Exiles* of James Joyce," in *Politics and Letters*, 1 (1948), pp. 13 ff.
62. E., pp. 288 ff., 326–8.

THE SANE AND JOYFUL SPIRIT: *ULYSSES*

The threads of Joyce's career all converged on *Ulysses*: Dublin, self-portraiture, his meditations on art, his evolving conception of drama. These now brought him to wider and more complex questions than ever. What was the "life" towards which he had always been groping? What could "freedom" and "maturity" mean in the modern world? Clearly, this new exploration of his experience would be, like his earlier ones, more a drama of understanding than of deeds. In the *Portrait* he had achieved a sharp but sympathetic irony; what would appear when he looked with the same poised understanding not only at himself but also at his society?

The answer is *Ulysses*, in which he achieved his youthful ideal of "the perfect manner in art"—what he had called "comedy" because it embraced the whole of life, including even its tragedy, and because it contemplated it steadily, in a spirit of "joy."[1] Once again he turned to the life he knew best and to the period from which his present mastery had grown. He now took for his subject every aspect he could see of one day—16 June 1904—in the life of Dublin. Stephen is now complemented by another, unexpected figure, Leopold Bloom—middle-aged, Jewish, canvasser for advertisements, notorious cuckold, a man struggling to come to terms with his not very accommodating world and with his jealousy of his all too accommodating wife—a commercial traveller to represent our age and to put beside the traveller of another age, Ulysses. The young potential artist looking for maturity, creativity, fatherhood, is now complemented

by the maturer citizen looking for a future, for under-
standing, a son. Stephen becomes Telemachus to Bloom's
Ulysses, Bloom becomes King Hamlet to Stephen's
Prince.

To portray them, Joyce developed the same method he
had used in the *Portrait*, and he used it again for much the
same reasons. Both heroes are now represented to us
through their "stream of consciousness"—that is (to put
it more accurately) through the acts of mind by which
they shape and order reality in the very process of ex-
periencing it. And once again the artist's own acts, the
understanding of the world which he now embodies in
shaping and ordering his experience into an *artistic*
reality, are an essential element of the drama.

The basic idea looks more complex than it is. To grasp
it we need only compare Joyce with his own exemplar.
Shakespeare's vision of the world in *Hamlet* is partly
Hamlet's own, partly the King's, and Horatio's, and
Ophelia's, and so on; but it is larger and deeper than any
because it includes them all—that is to say, because it
includes all that the characters do and say as objectively
understood elements in a pattern *they* cannot perceive.
Just so, Joyce's vision is partly Stephen's and Bloom's and
Molly Bloom's and that of all the other figures in the
book; but it is finally larger than any because he too is
"all in all."[2]

One difference between Shakespeare and Joyce,
however, is that Joyce insists that his total vision arose
out of the partial, limited vision of his characters, that it
actually grew out of the Dublin–1904 he portrays in his
book. Significantly, this is just what Stephen tries to
"prove" about Shakespeare and the situation in *Hamlet*
too. But whatever we think of that theory (and we need
not believe a word of it) the point is the same: while
Stephen talks about *Hamlet* he is really talking about
himself, and while he does that, Joyce is speaking
through him about *Ulysses*. Thus Joyce insists on the

reality of the *Ulysses*-world—it occupies a place and a
time real in the same sense that Joyce in Paris and
Zürich was real, or the novel itself is real as we hold it in
our hands. He insists on this because the book, as a
creative seven-year act of understanding (Trieste-Zürich-
Paris, 1914–21) did grow out of the world it portrays
(Dublin–1904). We see Stephen in it already looking to
the time when he will have grown able to see himself
(like Shakespeare) as he is now but in the light of what
he will have then become.[3] We see in Bloom a clear
representation of the world Stephen will both have to
experience in order to grow, and have to understand in
order to see what his maturity means. On the other hand,
of course, the world of *Ulysses* is not real, for it is a fiction
created and ordered by Joyce's imagination. And he
insists on this fact too—by his varied and unusual
techniques, by his parallels with the *Odyssey* and *Hamlet*
and other stories, by his network of symbols and references, by his shifting viewpoint, by his continual juxta-
positions of events. He insists on it because his present
moral and social understanding of Dublin–1904, the
insights and judgments embodied in his artistic ordering,
were not and could not have been available to anybody
in Dublin–1904. His "artifice" is the means by which he
can portray what his characters cannot perceive about
their own experience because they are too limited to see
it. His total vision (which becomes ours) is the measure
of theirs.

In this lies his major point about life and about art.
For Joyce, the human spirit is always embodied in a
particular "now and here," and therefore unable to
comprehend itself fully. Hence our need of the artist. But,
however confused and imperfect the ordinary world may
be, it is the soil in which our values live and in which
they must be rooted. It always contains, within its confusions and imperfections, the seeds of those humane
values which the greatest art, for example, can both

portray and embody in itself. If life, as Joyce now saw it, is always less than ideal, it is more than a chaos of impulse and delusion. Here then was his main task: to show all this in the world of Leopold Bloom and Stephen Dedalus—"to bend upon these present things and so to work upon them and fashion them that the quick intelligence may go beyond them to their meaning which is still unuttered. In this method the sane and joyful spirit issues forth and achieves imperishable perfection."[4]

Perfection, we must conclude, is too much to claim for *Ulysses*; the "sane and joyful spirit," however, is not; indeed, it is in this that its artistic power and importance really lie. It is a highly complicated work, patterned and woven so meticulously that whole books have been devoted to its mere mechanics. In some degree it is a critical analysis of modern society, a parody of cliché and confusion so pointed that other books have been devoted to the force of its attack. And yet what finally matters is neither its elaborate artifice nor its critical representation of our everyday chaos. Joyce's imagination reveals its power in the same way as he knew other artists' reveal theirs—in the quality of his evocation of *life*. This is much more than a matter of his "realism" or his suggestive "symbolism" or his clever tricks with the "stream of consciousness."[5] The relative absence of authorial comment, the apparently direct transcription of inner experience, the recurrent images, the abrupt "cutting," and so forth, do not make his art "dramatic" in any sense that really matters, nor did Joyce suppose they did. These conventions (they are nothing more) help to achieve an immediacy of effect, and they are devices necessary to an inward drama of understanding such as this. In themselves, however, they have no great importance. Much more important is the moral reality they help make substantial and alive. And once we grow accustomed to Joyce's conventions we can see that *Ulysses* comes alive not in its devices but in the very texture and order of its action. What is most important in the book is the vivid, ranging, deeply-felt and yet precisely-controlled vitality it reveals and embodies *within* the apparent chaos. And what goes with that: its comic verve, its subtle drama, the gradual emergence of its controlling vision from *within* its engagement with "the now, the here," as we are led eventually to see how the living spirit in Stephen and in Bloom and finally in Joyce himself (limited as each one is) are all real and all related.

Of the three we meet Stephen first, and it is quickly obvious in the opening chapters that *his* spirit is far from sane and joyful. He has not reached the goal he set out for at the end of the *Portrait*. As he himself realises (and as we might have expected) the furthest Icarus has got is "Newhaven–Dieppe, steerage passenger. Paris and back." He is "seabedabbled, fallen, weltering."[6] His mother has died and his conscience ("agenbite of inwit") haunts him with his conscientious refusal to pray at her death-bed. His family cannot help him nor he it. His friends—especially the ebullient, shallow Mulligan—are willing only to exploit him. He has produced nothing and has nothing much to produce from. While he struggles to protect himself against the personality his friends would foist on him (the tattered, sardonic Irish clown, "Kinch the Knifeblade"), he struggles, Hamlet-like, to come to terms with himself. He is, in short, in a remarkable state of Romantic *kinesis*: immature, bitter, mistrustful, insecure, egotistical, and frustrated, though with his intelligence and his dedication intact.

The opening chapters render his world with perfect exactness. As he apprehends it, it is cold, inimical, constricting. Its objects seem pregnant with hidden, perhaps ominous, significance ("signatures"); but it is a significance he is unable to read clearly. Occasionally, violent emotional disturbances rock, or even shatter, his vision altogether. "Gothic" images of death, "heroic" impulses,

F

sentimental self-pity, defensive bitterness, all tend to
break his experience into two quite unrelated areas—
what he sees and what he feels. Inevitably, his values
tend to lack substance and his vision objectivity.

And yet if he is still not the artist he wants to become
he is no longer the naïve idealist of the *Portrait*. He is a
stage further on, for he has at least been forced to
recognise the difficulties, the limitations, in his way. He
knows more than he did, and he is trying to do something
about it. He is prepared to venture forth again: in the
very first chapter he disgustedly gives Mulligan the key
to their "home," and at the end, when he leaves Bloom's
house, he has begun his second journey. But now he goes
with a rather deeper understanding of what achieving
"freedom" and "life" might involve. He goes "to seek
misfortune,"[7] to "act. Be acted on";[8] he has learned to
patiently trust time and experience to bring him to the
self he "must come to, ineluctably."[9]

He is now mature enough for Joyce to make him reflect
the wider issues involved in his case. His speculations on
history in the second chapter ("Nestor")[10] focus the
central issue—whether there is any direction and meaning in the flux of time, in human action and suffering.
Stephen realises the alternatives. Perhaps there is no
meaning to be discovered, and history merely a "tale
like any other too often heard,"[11] full only of "those big
words which make us so unhappy."[12] On the other hand,
perhaps there is a meaning to be created, and history a
process of fulfilment, a freeing of possibilities in life by the
active will of men and women—what he calls "an
actuality of the possible as possible."[13] That he accepts
the latter view is the first real sign of "the possible," the
potential life, in him. He thinks of the Jews, their "exile"
and their "patience":

. . . Vain patience to heap and hoard. Time surely
would scatter all. A hoard heaped by the roadside:

plundered and passing on. Their eyes knew the years
of wandering and, patient, knew the dishonours of their
flesh.

—Who has not? Stephen said.

—What do you mean? Mr Deasy asked.

He came forward a pace and stood by the table. His
underjaw fell sideways open uncertainly. Is this old
wisdom? He waits to hear from me.

—History, Stephen said, is a nightmare from which
I am trying to awake.

From the playfield the boys raised a shout. A whirr-
ing whistle: goal. What if that nightmare gave you a
back kick?

—The ways of the Creator are not our ways, Mr
Deasy said. All history moves towards one great goal,
the manifestation of God.

Stephen jerked his thumb towards the window,
saying:

—That is God.

Hooray! Ay! Whrrwhee!

—What? Mr Deasy asked.

—A shout in the street, Stephen answered, shrugging
his shoulders.[14]

His shrug is not cynicism but the admission of his limited
understanding. He sees that the one great goal of history
is the active fulfilment of human life itself—which is, if
we like, "the manifestation of God"—and it may take
the form of a deed, or a work of art (like *Hamlet*), or a
boy's or a drunken soldier's shout in the street. But how
can he know what any of these means unless he feels and
understands the life it expresses, unless *he* awakens into
life from the nightmare? That is the question he confronts
all through the novel. And when he does hear a shout in
the street later on (in "Circe," the episode in the brothel)
it accompanies a crucial insight he glimpses for the first
time: that Bloom, the representative of the society

Stephen rejects, embodies the same "life" as he is seeking.

Outside the gramophone begins to blare The Holy City.

STEPHEN

[*Abruptly*.] What went forth to the ends of the world
to traverse not itself. God, the sun, Shakespeare, a
commercial traveller, having itself traversed in reality
itself, becomes that self. Wait a moment. Wait a second.
Damn that fellow's noise in the street. Self which it
itself was ineluctably preconditioned to become.
Ecco![15]

It is significant of Stephen's condition, and characteristic
of Joyce's irony, that the young man can only reject the
noise in the street at the very moment when, as the
possible life in Bloom hovers on the edge of his understanding, he takes a step towards seeing its relation to
himself—a step ultimately towards Joyce's own understanding of this very moment of insight. *Ulysses* constantly judges the life it portrays by the significance
implied in the very portrayal.

But two chapters in particular are crucial for our view
of Stephen: "Proteus" (his walk on the seashore) and
"Scylla and Charybdis" (the Shakespeare discussion in
the library). In both of these the life growing in him is
vividly and unmistakably present, and it is here that we
see this other, less obvious side of him. In both he is
groping towards self-understanding. In the former, we
experience his inspection of his own past as he walks
along the edge of the "sea of life"; we feel his world from
within. In the other, we have the "external" counterpart:
his theory about art and life.

"Proteus" is like an embryonic version of the *Portrait*,
a critical, ironic self-scrutiny. The first thing we notice,
however, is that the writing is now more subtle, flexible
and concrete than it was earlier—or could have been.
The reality grasped (and ordered) by Stephen's con-

sciousness is more complex and more vividly present as
Stephen himself is more complexly and more vividly
alive. He begins with the ineluctable realities of "the
now, the here":

> Signatures of all things I am here to read, seaspawn
> and seawrack, the nearing tide, that rusty boot. Snot-
> green, bluesilver, rust: coloured signs . . .[16]

This is the physical world which, as he now realises, is
the only "signature" of its meaning. It is "there all the
time without you: and ever shall be, world without end";
it has to be accepted, reckoned with, in its physicality or
he will "knock his sconce" against it. From this he passes
to the visible and audible manifestations not of the
external world but of his own self—the stages of his
growth as he can now look back upon them and judge.
And at last he realises that he must seek his "father"
again on the dangerous "sea," despite his fear of falling
and drowning. Who knows? he may even enjoy it.[17]

But both the world without and the world within him
now have a greater energy than he ever possessed in the
Portrait. Not only has he this greater capacity for self-
mockery, for example, but even a casual act of observation shows a new liveliness in the liveliness he can grasp:

> Cocklepickers. They waded a little way in the water
> and, stooping, soused their bags, and, lifting them
> again, waded out. The dog yelped running to them,
> reared up and pawed them, dropping on all fours,
> again reared up at them with mute bearish fawning.
> Unheeded he kept by them as they came towards the
> drier sand, a rag of wolf's tongue redpanting from his
> jaws. His speckled body ambled ahead of them and
> then loped off at a calf's gallop. The carcass lay on his
> path. He stopped, sniffed, stalked round it, brother,
> nosing closer, went round it, sniffing rapidly like a dog
> all over the dead dog's bedraggled fell. Dogskull, dog-

sniff, eyes on the ground, moves to one great goal. Ah, poor dogsbody. Here lies poor dogsbody's body.

—Tatters! Out of that, you mongrel.[18]

The vitality lies not only in Stephen's ironic self-identification with the dog (an irony we relish with him); it lies in the keen, comic responsiveness of his whole vision. And the art, by which Joyce makes both Stephen and his world so substantially alive as they sniff about their dead past, characteristically embodies that comprehension of life (Stephen's and even the dog's) which is their "one great goal."

In the library episode Stephen is more obviously the kinetic young man. As in other scenes, he appears much more bitter and uneasy whenever he has to "knock his sconce" against the physical reality of other people. That, of course, is his basic trouble: as in the *Portrait*, he cannot come to terms with Dublin until he has come to terms with himself. His one advantage now is that he has become quite conscious of his central problem: the split between inner and outer, what he feels and what he sees.[19] His Shakespeare theory is his attempt to clarify it to himself and to work out a solution. Like Shakespeare, he, too, is "banished from the heart, banished from home,"[20] by both personal and social problems he cannot master. He, too, can win freedom only by acquiring the maturity to understand his bondage, and to break it in a deeper, more joyful, more inclusive mode of living: in art perhaps. Although he seems, therefore, at first a sad sack beside the high-spirited Mulligan, what we see of his inner world reveals how much further his problems and his impulses go. When it comes, his laughter means much more. As he finishes expounding his theory, he does laugh, "to free his mind from his mind's bondage."[21] The self-critical laugh, the theory it both concludes and illustrates, the inability of this one laugh to free him, Joyce's ironic smile at his inability to free himself as yet, and the relation between the laugh and the smile, all coalesce in the one moment.

So that Stephen can only glimpse what the day eventually offers him in Bloom. A man unconsciously seeking the statement, the ratification, of what he represents and what he finally *is*, Bloom—if Stephen could only see it—is his proper material as a novelist. In many ways he is even a model of Stephen's proper relations with his society. And in his limited, inarticulate vitality, he is also the ultimate reason for art itself. Appropriately, Bloom walks out of the library between Stephen and Mulligan, just as Stephen is resolving to part from his former friend and to seek what he must become; as he sees Bloom's back disappear he reaches a moment of genuine patience.[22] Consciously, however, he gets no further than the flash in "Circe," where he stumbles upon his insight about "God, the sun, Shakespeare, a commercial traveller." When, together with Bloom, he gazes into a mirror, he can see there only the *paralysed* face of "William Shakespeare."[23] As they sit together later on, he stumbles upon a further truth, and again fails to understand it: "*Christus* or Bloom his name is, or, after all, any other, *secundum carnem.*"[24]

But of course neither Bloom nor Stephen can really see what each means to the other. They could do so only if Bloom had Stephen's imaginative capacities and Stephen had Bloom's experience and detachment. The most they find in one another is a projection of their present selves. Bloom sees more deeply than Stephen; but only Joyce and we, who know what else there is in Bloom besides the "accumulation of the past" and know more of Stephen's future than Bloom can imagine,[25] are able to comprehend the relationships finally stated in the abstract terms of "Ithaca":

Did Stephen participate in his dejection?
He affirmed his significance as a conscious rational

animal proceeding syllogistically from the known to the unknown and a conscious rational reagent between a micro- and a macrocosm ineluctably constructed upon the incertitude of the void.

Was this affirmation apprehended by Bloom?

Not verbally. Substantially.

What comforted his misapprehension?

That as a competent keyless citizen he had proceeded energetically from the unknown to the known through the incertitude of the void. . . .[26]

Both then were silent?

Silent, each contemplating the other in both mirrors of the reciprocal flesh of theirhisnothis fellowfaces.[27]

When Stephen leaves Bloom, therefore, he has to go wandering through the very world in which Bloom has wandered. He has to become himself—first the young artist, eventually the author who sees him now by the light of what he has become. The lack of understanding between Stephen and Bloom, their inarticulate impulse towards each other, their differences and separation, their similarities and hidden kinship—all the paradoxical relationships caught up in the metaphor of "son and father"—sum up the tragic, comic relationships between life as it is and life as it aspires to be. On the one hand there are the confusions of "the now, the here"; on the other, the values to which it gropes and of which art is the symbol; and the imperfect life of both "son" and "father" fills the void between them.

Leopold Bloom represents what Stephen lacks, and in the book as a whole, he stands as the major comment on Stephen. Yet Bloom cannot be said fully to represent "life" either in the normative, moral sense of that term or in its descriptive, social sense, for he represents it in both and therefore represents each imperfectly. As he wanders through his society, he is continually and revealingly engaged in it—hence, of course, the Odyssean parallel. But his very immersion in the present, and the nature of the society he represents, both limit him drastically. The profounder, more comprehensive moral understanding that Stephen seeks, and which is present to us in the book as a whole, becomes in turn the major comment on Bloom.

If it is in Bloom that the comic vitality of the book most obviously resides, it is not simply in Bloom as a kind of ideal figure. It is rather in what Joyce reveals *in* him and *through* him, in the potentialities and the meaning he contains. For the spirit with which Joyce treats both his heroes is neatly caught in two small but far from casual observations, one given to Stephen, the other to Bloom. Stephen quotes St Augustine to himself:

It was revealed to me that those things are good which yet are corrupted which neither if they were supremely good nor unless they were good could be corrupted. . . .[28]

It is only the sane and joyful Joyce who sees the full truth of that in the Dublin Stephen is still, even as he quotes this, unable to accept. Similarly, it is only Joyce who can see the full meaning of Bloom's insight: that "in the midst of death we are in life."[29] Only Joyce is able to reveal, even in the Bloom who sees this in his own experience, an illustration of its truth. But this same outlook, and the balanced irony that rests upon it and serves it, are what "comedy" means in *Ulysses*.

On the one hand, Bloom clearly represents the prevailing "death" of Dublin–1904: a humble, confused, very ordinary man, embodying the commercialism, the rootlessness, the pervasive materialism of his society, its lack of vital beliefs and institutions, its fragmentation, its subtle impotence, its latent violence and hysteria. In the nightmare of the brothel episode, when the hidden impulses of the day emerge, his political ideals speak for his world:

I stand for the reform of municipal morals and the plain ten commandments. New worlds for old. Union of all, jew, moslem and gentile. Three acres and a cow for all children of nature. Saloon motor hearses. Compulsory manual labour for all. All parks open to the public day and night. Electric dishscrubbers. Tuberculosis, lunacy, war and mendicancy must now cease. General amnesty, weekly carnival, with masked licence, bonuses for all, esperanto the universal brotherhood. No more patriotism of barspongers and dropsical impostors. Free money, free love and a free lay church in a free lay state. . . . (*The new nine muses* [*appear*], *Commerce, Operatic Music, Amor, Publicity, Manufacture, Liberty of Speech, Plural Voting, Gastronomy, Private Hygiene, Seaside Concert Entertainments, Painless Obstetrics and Astronomy for the People.*)[30]

In his person, his thoughts, his situation, he embodies the familiar crisis of our age. As Disraeli put it over a century ago, "in great cities men are brought together by the desire of gain. They are not in a state of co-operation, but of isolation, as to the making of fortunes; and for the rest they are careless of neighbours. Christianity teaches us to love our neighbour as ourself; modern society acknowledges no neighbour." But Bloom is doubly, trebly isolated. As a converted Hungarian Jew, he is cut off from his racial past and yet not an Irishman; his father committed suicide in despair; his only son, Rudy, died in childhood; his daughter, Milly, has left home; and not only is he sexually cut off from his wife, Molly, but he knows that she is unfaithful, that in fact she will be meeting her current lover, Blazes Boylan, on this very afternoon. He is snubbed and mocked. Loneliness and self-pity threaten him all day and erupt at last in the wild, impotent fantasies of "Circe."

He seems able to do little more than suffer his world as its passive victim, to evoke only pathos. His senses

constantly suffer its ugly chaos. He suffers its evasive
sloth in "Lotus-eaters," for example; its windy rhetoric
in "Aeolus"; its deadened feelings in "Hades"; its
ruthless physicality in "Lestrygonians"; its atomisation
in "Wandering Islands"; the blur of its noise in "Sirens";
its political weakness in "Cyclops"; and so on. His
reactions seem little more than a focus of the prevailing
chaos. Thus in "Nausicaa" he suffers the vicious, crippled,
"girlish" sexiness of Gerty MacDowell; his reaction,
appropriately enough, is to masturbate. Time itself
seems only a dimension of suffering, a nightmare from
which he cannot awake. The future holds nothing:

> I too, last my race. Milly young student. Well, my fault
> perhaps. No son. Rudy. . . . Soon I am old.[31]

The present, as he sits lunching, offers to his gaze two
flies copulating on the windowpane, while he remembers
the ecstatic joy of his first meetings with his wife: "She
kissed me. I was kissed. All yielding she tossed my hair.
Kissed, she kissed me. Me. And me now."[32] He turns to
thoughts of the immortal beauty of art, in which human
passion seems transcended and given another meaning;
but he can make almost nothing of it.[33] When he is
suddenly confronted with the figure of Boylan in the
street, he bolts blindly into the Museum.[34] The "cold
statues" of "the Greek architecture" offer him only a
temporary retreat from a past and a present equally
unbearable but to which he is ineluctably bound. The
conventionalities in which he is immersed, the *idées
reçues* which Joyce parodies so ruthlessly (and amusingly),
only heighten the pathos of his condition. He can com-
municate with Stephen only through a thick soup of
cliché. He is helpless and inarticulate. He tries to write a
message in the sand: "What? I. . . . AM. A. No room. Let
it go. . . . Hopeless thing sand. Nothing grows in it. All
fades."[35]

Nevertheless, whatever he may seem, Bloom is very

far from a simple mixture of Bouvard and Pécuchet, Babbitt, and The Little Man.[36] He is not merely the helpless bourgeois trapped within his sterile society any more than Stephen is merely the Romantic artist correspondingly trapped within his isolated and sterile ego. Certainly, these do form one aspect of each of them, and in both we can discover a social criticism that has been made time and again through the nineteenth and twentieth centuries. Nevertheless, there is more to Stephen than this, and a great deal more to Bloom.

For one thing, Bloom possesses moral virtues that isolate him from his society in another sense altogether. He is kind, as well as prudent, courageous, just, magnanimous, a man whose *habit* is good, and whose actions —though they are necessarily limited in scope—*do* acknowledge his neighbours. He goes out of his way to help the family of a dead acquaintance, for example, and it is (appropriately enough) while he is doing so that he is led to speak up against the crippled, violent chauvinism of "the Citizen." While the others in the pub are silent, Bloom's action represents what awaking from the nightmare of history might mean:

—But it's no use, says he [Bloom]. Force, hatred, history, all that. That's not life for men and women, insult and hatred. And everybody knows that it's the very opposite of that that is really life.
—What? says Alf.
—Love, says Bloom. I mean the opposite of hatred. . . .[37]

He cannot articulate what he means. Inevitably, the debased language he has to use ("Love") is misunderstood, and inevitably he talks too much and is himself misunderstood. But both the corruption and the good are there, and in the ironic comedy of Joyce's prose both are ratified. Enraged by Bloom's intransigence, by his shocking suggestion that Christ was a Jew, and above all by his failure to stand a round of drinks when he apparently ought, "the Citizen" characteristically hurls a biscuit-tin at the hurriedly departing prophet (and characteristically misses him):

> When, lo, there came about them all a great bright-ness and they beheld the chariot wherein He stood ascend to heaven. And they beheld Him in the chariot, clothed upon in the glory of the brightness, having raiment as of the sun, fair as the moon and terrible that for awe they durst not look upon Him. And there came a voice out of heaven, calling: *Elijah! Elijah!* And he answered with a main cry: *Abba! Adonai!* And they beheld Him even Him, ben Bloom Elijah, amid clouds of angels ascend to the glory of the brightness at an angle of fortyfive degrees over Donohoe's in Little Green Street like a shot off a shovel.[38]

This is the spirit in which Bloom is seen continuously. Even when he stands guard over the drunken Stephen— who has had his "sconce" literally knocked by the world of now and here—and beholds an appallingly sentimental "vision" of his dead son,[39] he is still a "secret master." As always, the joke on Bloom is fused with the recognition of his strength—a strength all the greater for his complete unawareness of it.

The one problem he is aware of all day is his jealousy of Molly, and perhaps nothing reveals his essential maturity (and Joyce's growth since *Exiles*) more than the way he gradually brings himself to confront and accept the facts and to see his own part in the situation. Characteristically, he emerges as both *cocu voulu* and "unconquered hero,"[40] at once absurd, pathetic, and indefeasibly sane. At first his reactions are purely kinetic: panic, self-pity, evasion. Slowly, he begins to save himself: "Stop. Stop. If it was it was. Must," he thinks, and (significantly) passes "Adam Court."[41] Later on he recognises something more: "He bore no hate.

Hate. Love. Those are names. Rudy. Soon I am old."[42] In "Nausicaa" his patient, compassionate understanding can be felt in the very rhythms of his thought.[43] Later, the brothel evokes his latent desires as gibbering visions: his secret wish to be betrayed, his masochism, his desire to be a social Messiah and create perfect Justice, his secret dread of his society and wish to be merely its innocent victim, his social and sexual guilt, and finally—the supreme test of his manhood—the deadly wish to flee from "the now, the here" into a soft, ethereal, ideal remoteness, to surrender all the complicating desire, all the compromised effort of living as a human being. He half rises to the spiritual bait.[44] Characteristically, he is saved by a comic accident: his highly physical back trousers' button snaps off. He regains his dignity; "composed," he is once again master of himself and at last he moves to the "silent contemplation," the moral *stasis*, summed up in "Ithaca." Here he has reached the patient sanity he has been seeking all day. More convincingly than the hero of *Exiles*, he has come to recognise and accept Molly's freedom as well as his own part in the failure of their relationship. He comes to a state of mind that is "more abnegation than jealousy, less envy than equanimity."[45] The returning Ulysses has killed his true enemies, which are (like Stephen's) those within.[46] Yet he remains alive in his own way to the end. His silent contemplation of Molly has none of the permanence, but none of the fixity, of aesthetic *stasis*. Once again, Joyce's writing catches, even as its comic irony transcends, Bloom's absurd, irrepressible vitality:

He kissed the plump mellow yellow smellow melons of her rump, on each plump melonous hemisphere, in their mellow yellow furrow, with obscure prolonged provocative melonsmellonous osculation.[47]

But Bloom's moral vitality extends to more than his obvious moral deeds and decisions. His mind is constantly alive, critically alive, to his surroundings and even at times to himself. His moral values inform his very apprehension of the world, enabling him not merely to suffer it but actively to understand it and, in understanding, to criticise. If *Ulysses* is Joyce's critical understanding of the modern world, of Bloom himself, it is also Bloom who most represents Joyce, who initiates the criticism that Joyce completes. Bloom's, we might say, is the Primary Imagination of humanity in the book; Joyce's the Secondary Imagination of the artist, working through the former but going beyond it.

A passage from "Hades"—as a whole, one of the finest episodes in the book—may offer a small representative example. Each of the four mourners in the carriage is entombed in a private world of pain and distress; even more than the dead Paddy Dignam, they embody—individually and collectively—the social "breakdown," the "broken heart," which forms the theme of the whole episode. And Bloom, of course, isolated still further by his race and his cuckoldry, seems at first the purest embodiment of all. Yet the drama takes on a far deeper significance as it recalls his father's suicide, Martin Cunningham's drunkard wife, Mr Dedalus' cowardly evasion of his family responsibilities, and Mr Power's "disgraceful" affair with a barmaid.

The carriage climbed more slowly the hill of Rutland square. Rattle his bones. Over the stones. Only a pauper. Nobody owns.

—In the midst of life, Martin Cunningham said.

—But the worst of all, Mr Power said, is the man who takes his own life.

Martin Cunningham drew out his watch briskly, coughed and put it back.

—The greatest disgrace to have in the family, Mr Power added.

—Temporary insanity, of course, Martin Cunning-

ham said decisively. We must take a charitable view
of it.

—They say a man who does it is a coward, Mr
Dedalus said.

—It is not for us to judge, Martin Cunningham
said.

Mr Bloom about to speak, closed his lips again.
Martin Cunningham's large eyes. Looking away now.
Sympathetic human man he is. Intelligent. Like Shakespeare's face. Always a good word to say. They have
no mercy on that here or infanticide. Refuse christian
burial. They used to drive a stake of wood through his
heart in the grave. As if it wasn't broken already. Yet
sometimes they repent too late. Found in the riverbed
clutching rushes. He looked at me. And that awful
drunkard of a wife of his. Setting up house for her time
after time and then pawning the furniture on him
every Saturday almost. Leading him the life of the
damned. Wear the heart out of a stone, that. Monday
morning start afresh. Shoulder to the wheel. Lord, she
must have looked a sight that night, Dedalus told me
he was in there. Drunk about the place and capering
with Martin's umbrella:

> And they call me the jewel of Asia,
> Of Asia,
> The geisha.

He looked away from me. He knows. Rattle his
bones.[48]

The children's rhyme running in Bloom's thoughts is
like a text whose meaning is explored in the different
areas of experience Bloom brings together, both in what
he thinks and what he is. The conventional attitude to
suicide is seen for what it is—"heartless," un-self-aware;
the heartbreak and the loneliness that cause suicide are
felt in the private Hell of the living; Cunningham's
sympathy for Bloom is suggestively juxtaposed with

Shakespeare's, the artist's; old Virag-Bloom's pathetic desolation is placed beside the individual's rights which "nobody owns" but himself; every man's ultimate alone-ness gives point to Bloom's responsive but critical understanding of the others and their values, an understanding greater than Cunningham's because including him; and all these become part of Joyce's comprehension of the whole scene, including Bloom himself, whose heart is alone but visibly alive "in the midst of death."

Throughout *Ulysses*, the greater part of Stephen's and Bloom's activity is, like this, "mental" rather than "physical"; but it is activity none the less. They observe, think, relate, and order, and in doing so, they judge. By his "stream of consciousness" technique Joyce is able to represent these inward actions dramatically, and by doing so he expresses two of his fundamental insights. The first is the more obvious: we are made to *feel* the isolation, the helplessness even, of the individual in modern society in the lonely, fragmented quality of his experience. But we feel more than that. For the second insight is that, inasmuch as a man's freedom is a condition of his spirit, an essential rationality, a harmony and justice in his soul (for it is just these worn old tags whose life Joyce is seeking amid the rubbish of history), this freedom is to be found in what he makes of the world inwardly more perhaps than in what he does to it outwardly. It will lie in his critical responsiveness to, but detachment from, his immediate present.

Looked at carefully, Joyce's "stream of consciousness" is not what it is usually taken to be—a mere photographic copy, so to speak, of the chaotic "impressions" or "images" passively received by the mind or welling up out of the Unconscious.[49] It is rather, as I have suggested, the artistic rendering of a mind engaged in apprehending its world, and *enacting its values* in the very process of apprehending. And as we can see even in this brief example it depends on certain conventions. For one thing, it depends on the convention of ordinary, third-person, "omniscient" narrative: we have to see the character from "outside" as well as experience the quality of his world from "within." But it also depends on a convention of Joyce's own, one that is often overlooked: simply, that the *paragraph* forms the dramatic unit and is the artistic medium of a particular *act* of understanding. As Joyce uses it, the paragraph embodies both an act of the character's "soul," an act that expresses his values in the way he grasps some part of his world, and at the same time the inner shape of that world as he grasps it. In other words, it is a mature version of what Joyce had once called the "epiphany"—in which what one sees and what one feels, fact and value, are fused in an act of understanding.

Here, of course, this is only one element in the more complex drama at Joyce's command. As "Hades" progresses, for example, we experience all that the funeral and the conventional clichés about death mean in Bloom's varied, compassionate, limited, sensible, pathetic, humorous acts of understanding: the violent egotism coexisting in old Dedalus with genuine love of his son,[50] or the feeble "heart" of the city through which they pass,[51] or the connexions between death and sex,[52] or the difference between the grief expressed—or rather, paralysed —in sentimental stone and bronzefoil and that expressed in real flowers that live and die.[53] Although Bloom is obviously part of the "deadness" around him, his experience gradually makes us feel, and Joyce's narrative gradually leads us to see, how he also realises (in the sense that includes embodies) the life in the midst of that death. It is not only his overt actions that matter but his very style, so to speak:

The gates glimmered in front: still open. Back to the world again. Enough of this place. Brings you a bit nearer every time. Last time I was here was Mrs

Sinico's funeral. Poor papa too. The love that kills. And even scraping up the earth at night with a lantern like that case I heard of to get at fresh buried females or even putrefied with running gravesores. Give you the creeps after a bit. I will appear to you after death. You will see my ghost after death. My ghost will haunt you after death. There is another world after death named hell. I do not like that other world she wrote. No more do I. Plenty to see and hear and feel yet. Feel live warm beings near you. Let them sleep in their maggoty beds. They are not going to get me this innings. Warm beds: warm fullblooded life.[54]

Once again we feel the strength even while we remember that he himself is hardly a prime example of the full-blooded and that his bed is occasionally warmed by Blazes Boylan.

But a large range of Dublin is focused in this way by Bloom—not merely, as it seems at first sight, by what he suffers, but also in what he sees and judges. He is detached from his society as well as immersed in it; what he sees, he sees straight. Thus while the Dubliners in the newspaper office are orating about War, History, Justice for Ireland, and so on, Bloom observes the machines that help carry their ideals through the whole of society: "working away, tearing away":[55] "Justice it means but it's everybody eating everyone else. That's what life is after all."[56] He constantly places the society he observes against his sense of what it ought to be: its sloth and evasion, its empty rhetoric and sentimentality, its brutality, its injustice. Its fragmentation and his judgment on it are both made vividly present:

His smile faded as he walked, a heavy cloud hiding the sun slowly, shadowing Trinity's surly front. Trams passed one another, ingoing, outgoing, clanging. Useless words. Things go on same; day after day: squads of police marching out, back: trams in, out. Those two

loonies mooching about. Dignam carted off. Mina
Purefoy swollen belly on a bed groaning to have a
child tugged out of her. One born every second somewhere. Other dying every second. Since I fed the birds
five minutes. Three hundred kicked the bucket. Other
three hundred born, washing the blood off, all are
washed in the blood of the lamb, bawling maaaaaa.

Cityful passing away, other cityful coming, passing
away too: other coming on, passing on. Houses, lines
of houses, streets, miles of pavements, piledup bricks,
stones. Changing hands. This owner, that. Landlord
never dies they say. Other steps into his shoes when he
gets his notice to quit. They buy the place up with gold
and still they have all the gold. Swindle in it somewhere. Piled up in cities, worn away age after age.
Pyramids in sand. Built on bread and onions. Slaves.
Chinese wall. Babylon. Big stones left. Round towers.
Rest rubble, sprawling suburbs, jerrybuilt, Kerwan's
mushroom houses, built of breeze. Shelter for the night.

No one is anything.

This is the very worst hour of the day. Vitality. Dull,
gloomy: hate this hour. Feel as if I had been eaten and
spewed.[57]

The easy, casual turn of self-critical awareness at the end
qualifies his judgment, as it must; the passage as a whole
is a perfect illustration of the concreteness, the objectivity, the sanity, the recognition of self, towards which
Stephen has started groping.

Bloom's judgments are never utopian and never bitter.
In "Circe," his nature prevents him from being swallowed
up in any simplification of his essential humanity. He is
neither social Messiah nor social martyr; being part of
his world, but not entirely part of it, he is always forced
back to being himself as he is—a man unwilling to wound
the human dignity of a whore, able to accept the
"necessary evils" of life with human grace, responsive to

both the pain and the value of human growth.[58] He represents something far deeper and more complex than his fantasies or impotence; and in "Circe" he gets free of them at least sufficiently for us to glimpse the irreducible, unfathomable core of his being. His is the humanity that presents every society with its central problem and also with its measure.

The catechism of "Ithaca" places him for our final, impersonal judgment. Here, under the assault of the cold, "scientifically" objective intellect, his *petit-bourgeois* dreams are anatomised in their own crude jargon, his "ideals" festooned about him ludicrously. Yet, ironically, the very abstraction only serves to underline what cannot be reduced to such terms.[59] Once again the joke is not so much on Bloom as it *is* Bloom. Reduced to his basic elements, he still remains Everyman or Noman, the hidden Ulysses, "assumed by any or known to none."[60] In this harsh light we perceive the dark centre of life untouched, the spirit which has moved him all through and which justifies his "fatherhood" of Stephen: as the artist must too, he patiently accepts his world from within, indeed represents it, but remains sufficiently detached to seek what reaches beyond the local and particular. "In this method the sane and joyful spirit issues forth. . . ."

In this, of course, lies the chief strength of the third member of the Joycian trinity—the artist himself. As a work of art, *Ulysses* is most "sane and joyful" where it at once evokes, criticises, and celebrates the life in Stephen and Bloom and the world they share and represent. This is the real achievement of the book.

But, like his heroes', Joyce's artistic vitality is not uncompromised or perfect, and it calls for the same kind of critical understanding as he gives Stephen and Bloom. For, ironically, what limited him, too, was his occasional failure to understand what his own deepest inspiration really was, his inability, as we might put it, to awaken perfectly from his history. He was still dogged by the self-image of the "fabulous artificer," the technical virtuoso. And the result lies visible in the more superficial, mechanical, merely cerebral aspects of *Ulysses*, in the obvious, laborious "brilliance" that he over-valued—and that led many critics into over-valuing as well. Some of his critics, for instance, praise his devastating and encyclopaedic parody of modern values; others his elaborate texture of "symbols"; others seem intoxicated by his use of myths, archetypes, or the discoveries of modern psychology. The praise may not seem to us as flattering as it might have seemed to Joyce; all it does, in fact, is underline some of the most serious weaknesses of *Ulysses*.[61]

For it is almost a critical commonplace—even among some of Joyce's keenest admirers—that he laboured some things too much. What is more, he was inclined at times to take pattern for form, artifice for art, animus for animation. The elaborate time-scheme and geographical detail he included; the elaborate scheme of arts, organs of the body, colours, symbols, and "technics" he wove into all the episodes; the elaborate detail with which he worked in Homeric "parallels" and other "myths" like Robinson Crusoe, Don Giovanni, Sinbad, as well as *Hamlet* and the Bible; the elaborate parodies in which he mocks our cliché-ridden society; his evident desire to cover every aspect of life, to say everything he had to say in terms of this book, all point to weaknesses he mistook for strength. Or rather, perhaps, weaknesses that were inseparably bound up with his strength. For while these virtuosities call for criticism rather than praise, they also help us to understand some of the hard necessities under which he had to work.

If the necessary judgments are pretty obvious, therefore, they are not quite as uncomplicated as they may seem at first sight. Thus one of the things that makes *Ulysses* a literary monument of our age is its range, the fearless and inventive realism which justifies Joyce's claim that "if it isn't fit to read, life isn't fit to live";[62] and of this, as Hugh Kenner has said, the extrinsic patterns are partly the instrument.[63] On the other hand, *Ulysses* leaves out too much to make it the final, encyclopaedic epic it obviously aims to be—the fulfilment of the Symbolists' dream of an absolutely comprehensive "poem."[64] Its treatment of industrialism, class, sex, mass institutions, science, ideology, war (to look no further), reveals how much of modern life Joyce could not discover in his experience, in Dublin-1904. Again, it is as a whole too wide, too responsive to the facts it does perceive, too balanced, to be merely a comic epic *Waste Land* in prose, as some critics would wish it to be. On the other hand, it includes certain aspects of life only by lapsing into mere parody. In parts of "Cyclops," or "Nausicaa," "Eumaeus," or even "Ithaca," for example, the energy of the writing is largely destructive, and it is elaborated too wilfully to sustain our interest once we have taken the comparatively simple point it is making. Aiming only to mock, the art can hardly respond to the full complexity of life it reveals elsewhere: we need only compare the writing in the first section of "Nausicaa," for instance, where Gerty's sentimental romanticism is ruthlessly parodied, with the second part, where Bloom's complexly ironic condition is rendered, to see the basic rigidity of the one against the deeper vitality of the other. Where the parody *is* imaginatively right (as in ben Bloom Elijah's ascent to heaven or in parts of "Ithaca"), it depends for its effect upon the dramatic action; the mockery is balanced, and finally absorbed, by a fuller and richer attitude. But, as with *Dubliners*, where Joyce simply reveals emptiness or chaos for what it is, simply assumes the criteria of judgment without making them sensibly present in his art, his writing is imaginatively trapped in the very thing he wishes to reject. He had learned this lesson the hard way, but of course to achieve freedom is even harder, and neither he nor *Ulysses* is entirely free from the cruder "irony" of his earlier work.

Similarly with the other elements. The "mythic" parallels, the unusual techniques (the "gestation" analogy in "Oxen of the Sun," for instance, or the "music" analogy in "Sirens"), the recurrent "motifs" or "symbols," all involved Joyce in enormous labour, and they have provoked Joycian scholars to corresponding marvels of explication. But the "ideas" on which they are based are so thin, the "patterns" they create so superficial, that it is doubtful if in themselves they have any imaginative effect upon the reader—except perhaps to make him wonder why Joyce bothered. The answer to that, I believe, is again two-fold, and again we ought to understand Joyce's difficulties before dismissing his solution out of hand. On the one side, they are clearly part of his encyclopaedic ambition, an attempt to frame and co-ordinate his portrait of a society without any internal order of its own. For any modern artist, living within the confusion he portrays, it is hard to avoid arbitrary expedients, and the best Joyce could do was to give his such imaginative force as he could. The wonder is not that he failed; it is rather that the extrinsic patterns achieve any degree of meaning (as they do, more or less, up to about "Cyclops" and again in "Circe"), and, what is more, that their elaboration does not ruin the whole book. The reason, I believe, is that they also play a more important strategic role in the dramatic action. Crude, extrinsic, over-clever, sometimes downright silly as they are, these stylistic devices are finally less important than the real structure of the book, a structure that they partially serve.

At first sight, it may seem as if dramatic structure is just what *Ulysses* lacks. Stephen and Bloom act and react in their world, they meet and part, there is a temporal sequence of a sort, the Homeric pattern is completed, and so, too, is the circling panorama of arts, organs, and so forth; but there seems to be no meaningful development. In fact there is, but not in "what happens" in Dublin–1904. It lies rather in our developing view *of* Dublin–1904, in the emergence of our wider, more comprehensive understanding. Slowly we are moved from our immersion in the characters' present experience; gradually our awareness of what they represent, what they are potentially, and how they are related, accumulates and jells; and we begin less to see with them than through them, contemplating them now objectively as "cases," significant instances in a significant context. Joyce manoeuvres our vision until we understand the larger "drama" embodied in this "now and here." He leads his (and our) apprehension of this world towards comprehension of it. This kind of structure was quite essential to *Ulysses*; whatever Joyce thought to the contrary, however, the encyclopaedic coverage was not. We had to feel his moral vision was comprehensive in the sense that his values were large and sane enough to accommodate the seemingly contradictory facts of life; it was less important to feel that his understanding was comprehensive in the sense that it covered every department of life. But the two senses are so closely related that Joyce evidently felt he could (or must) compound them. To achieve his major end, therefore, to make us more and more conscious of his *moral* comprehension, he used the tactic of gently insisting on his constructive artifice and on the social criticism implicit in his increasingly sophisticated styles. He could not enter the book openly in his own person as earlier novelists had done; he wanted to portray Dublin–1904 entirely in its own terms, and his whole point was that he had been present in that world but only as a *potentiality*. Nevertheless, he had to make his mature presence dramatically felt somehow. To make his "artistry" actually obtrude on our notice was his solution.

It called for a tact, a delicate balance of means and ends, which obviously failed him at times: the self-conscious artifice, especially from "Cyclops" onwards, is often amusing but more often tends rather to exasperate.[65] Nevertheless, it achieves something. In "Cyclops," where *we* know what Bloom means by Love, he and his values are now explicitly placed hard against the mis-understanding, the maliciousness, the violence, the banality of his society, and all these are commented on by the enveloping parodies with a far greater sophistica-tion than Bloom could ever reach. In the following chapters, "Nausicaa" and "Oxen of the Sun," both Bloom and Stephen are increasingly seen as part of social and natural *forces*. The next chapter, "Circe," takes them quite objectively. Bloom is now treated in his representative aspect—both in what the nightmare of history could make of him and in what, after all, it can not; different planes of reality now collide and intersect and are finally merged in our more inclusive understand-ing of both "father" and "son." The last section of the book can therefore adopt a new stance towards its material: "the now, the here" is set in a wider, more general—and, we must notice, more abstract—perspec-tive. The social decay we have perceived is now summed up in the dreary clichés of "Eumaeus." In "Ithaca" the meaning of Stephen and Bloom can now be *stated*; and in this distant view of them, we can now see that, for all the sad differences between Bloom and Ulysses, their outlines at least do, after all, coincide. The apparently arbitrary Homeric parallel is founded in what we now, as we stand beyond the now and here, realise we have been witnessing in it all along. It is now plain that *Ulysses* does not merely retrace or re-enact the pattern of traditional myths. Its more difficult and more valuable achievement has been to re-discover their living sense, to re-create them. So that Joyce neither simply denies Bloom and Stephen and their world, nor simply "affirms" them. He reveals them for what they are: only partly coherent and free, limited, compromised, but nevertheless incarnations of the same spirit as "issues forth" in Ulysses, Shakespeare, God, and Joyce too, creating what order it can in the chaos of reality as it moves through it, so that, finally, it may possess itself more fully. What Joyce does affirm is this spirit of life, which is manifest not merely in traditional myths but also in the very creation of myths. Revealing its presence in Stephen and Bloom, Joyce offers the material, the motive, and the end of his art, his "myth," as he now sees it. Art is not his supreme value; it is—like the world he had now discovered in his fiction—only an embodiment of it in a particular now and here.

And so he concludes with Molly Bloom's silent monologue, with the teeming chaos out of which other possibilities, other forms and expressions of life, will arise. Molly is the recognition of his own limitations, the recognition that after all, despite its vast ambitions, *Ulysses* is only one act of self-comprehension and that the ironical truth it celebrates applies to itself as well. With this chapter, Joyce reached the utmost limits of his imaginative understanding—and we can see the void ahead reflected in it. To encompass the whole of what had been portrayed in *Ulysses*, to suggest what lay beneath and beyond the life he had so patiently scrutinised—the "prehuman" and the "posthuman" earth, as he put it[66] —he was forced upon a fatal degree of abstraction. As his perspective grew wider, the less it could discriminate, of course; but the abstraction of "Ithaca" is largely rooted in, grows from, and completes what has been enacted. In this last chapter it necessarily breaks away from the dramatic action. Molly has both to represent and to affirm Life with a capital L—"and yes I said yes I will Yes." Her artistic function, that is to say, is to affirm the possibility of *everything*. Her monologue is therefore necessarily formless, inchoate; but necessarily, too, it confuses all the subtle moral distinctions to which the whole book has been devoted. No wonder some critics take it as expressing the very heart of Dublin's "death."[67] Joyce wanted to have his cake and eat it too; but he could perform miracles only in theory. Hence the pervasive factitiousness of the writing, apart from the last thirty or so lines on which so much of the chapter's effect relies; and hence, I think, Molly's failure to achieve the vivid, substantial presence of Stephen or Bloom. Joyce had to be more concerned with the general idea Molly represents than with the specific quality of life embodied in his rendering of her. "The now, the here" had finally to be sacrificed to its formless essence.

If the *Portrait* was a turning-point in Joyce's career, *Ulysses* was its fruit. Here he brought together all his main concerns and placed them in relation to each other—the texture and shape of society, the place of the individual in it and his search for identity, the significance of art, the processes and values in which life consists. *Ulysses* shows us what these can mean to us, or at least part of what they can mean: where, that is to say, they are to be seen and felt in the writing. Therein lies its power, which ranks it among the major achievements of the modern novel. Even by comparison with Lawrence or Mann or Proust, for example, Joyce obviously achieves a very great deal. But he also wanted to do more, to discover "comic" joy in more than his imagination could really penetrate. And in reaching at the very end of *Ulysses* towards an all-embracing vision of Life itself, a Summa so complete that it would seem morally invulnerable, he perfected the self-defensive tactics of his earliest work, came at last to his earliest mistake, and reached another turning-point.

REFERENCES

1. *C.W.*, pp. 144–5.

2. *U.*, p. 200 (272; 210).

3. *Op. cit.*, p. 183 (249; 192).

4. *S.H.*, p. 83 (78).

5. For a survey of approaches to *Ulysses*, see Goldberg, *The Classical Temper*, chs. 1, 4, 6, 7. This discusses at greater length the reading of *Ulysses* offered here and the related critical issues. Also cp. Magalaner and Kain, *Joyce*, chs. 7–8.

For the "mechanics" see esp. F. Budgen, *James Joyce and the Making of Ulysses*, London 1937; S. Gilbert, *James Joyce's Ulysses*, rev. edn. London 1952; R. M. Kain, *Fabulous Voyager*, Chicago 1947. For the social criticism, Ezra Pound, *Literary Essays*, London 1954, pp. 403 ff.; Levin, *James Joyce*, pp. 65 ff.; D. Knight, "The Reading of *Ulysses*," in *ELH*, xix (1952), pp. 64 ff.; Kenner, *Dublin's Joyce*, pp. 158 ff. For the "symbolism," W. Y. Tindall, *James Joyce*. For the "stream of consciousness," R. Humphrey, *Stream of Consciousness in the Modern Novel*, Berkeley and Los Angeles 1954; M. Friedman, *Stream of Consciousness: A Study in Literary Method*, New Haven 1955, pp. 21 off.

6. *U.*, p. 199 (270; 208).

7. *Op. cit.*, p. 581 (713; 604).

8. *Op. cit.*, p. 199 (271; 208).

9. *Op. cit.*, pp. 47 (63–4; 51), 205–6 (279; 214).

10. The Homeric chapter-titles (which Joyce finally omitted) are useful for reference: 1. Telemachus; 2. Nestor; 3. Proteus; 4. Calypso; 5. Lotuseaters; 6. Hades; 7. Aeolus; 8. Lestrygonians; 9. Scylla and Charybdis; 10. Wandering Rocks; 11. Sirens; 12. Cyclops; 13. Nausicaa; 14. Oxen of the Sun; 15. Circe; 16. Eumaeus; 17. Ithaca; 18. Penelope.

11. *U.*, p. 22 (30; 26).

12. *Op. cit.*, p. 28 (38; 32).

13. *Op. cit.*, p. 23 (30; 26).

14. *Op. cit.*, pp. 31–2 (42; 35).

15. *Op. cit.*, p. 479 (623; 494).

16. *Op. cit.*, p. 33 (45; 38).

17. *Op. cit.*, p. 47 (63; 51).

18. *Op. cit.*, p. 43 (58; 47).

19. Cp. *op. cit.*, p. 229 (311; 238).

20. *Op. cit.*, p. 200 (272; 209).

21. Ibid.

22. *Op. cit.*, p. 206 (279; 215).

23. *Op. cit.*, p. 536 (671; 553).

24. *Op. cit.*, p. 604 (745; 627).

25. *Op. cit.*, p. 650 (807; 673).

26. *Op. cit.*, p. 658 (817–18; 682).

27. *Op. cit.*, p. 663 (824; 687).

28. *Op. cit.*, p. 132 (180; 140).

29. *Op. cit.*, p. 100 (136; 106).

30. *Op. cit.*, pp. 465–6 (610–11; 480).

31. *Op. cit.*, p. 270 (367–8; 280).

32. *Op. cit.*, p. 165 (224; 173).

33. *Op. cit.*, p. 165 (224–5; 174).

34. *Op. cit.*, pp. 171–2 (234; 180–1).

35. *Op. cit.*, p. 364 (497–8; 375).

36. Cp. E., p. 390 and Ellmann's "Ulysses the Divine No-body," in *Yale Review*, XLVII (1957), pp. 56 ff.; R. P. Blackmur's excellent "The Jew in Search of a Son," in *Virginia Quarterly Review*, XXIV (1948), pp. 96 ff.; E. Mason, "James Joyce, Moralist," in *Twentieth Century Literature*, I (1956), pp. 196 ff.

37. *U.*, p. 317 (432; 327).

38. *Op. cit.*, p. 329 (449; 339).

39. *Op. cit.*, p. 574 (702–3; 593).

40. *Op. cit.*, p. 251 (340; 260).

41. *Op. cit.*, p. 156 (212; 165).

42. *Op. cit.*, p. 270 (368; 280).

43. *Op. cit.*, pp. 359–60 (491; 370).

44. *Op. cit.*, p. 523 (661; 539).

45. *Op. cit.*, p. 694 (865; 718).

46. *Op. cit.*, p. 556 (688; 574).

47. *Op. cit.*, p. 695 (867; 719).

48. *Op. cit.*, pp. 88–9 (120–1; 95).

49. *E.g.* Kain, *Fabulous Voyager*, pp. 131 ff. Contrast E., p. 542.

50. *U.*, pp. 80–1 (109–10; 87–8).

51. *Op. cit.*, p. 88 (119; 94).

52. *Op. cit.*, pp. 99–100 (135–6; 106–7).

53. *Op. cit.*, p. 105 (143–4; 111–112).

54. *Op. cit.*, pp. 106–7 (145–6; 113).

55. *Op. cit.*, p. 110 (150; 117).

56. *Op. cit.*, p. 114 (155; 121).

57. *Op. cit.*, p. 153 (208; 162).

58. *Op. cit.*, pp. 475 (619; 489), 658 (817; 681).

59. Cp. Edmund Wilson, *Axel's Castle*, New York and London 1950, pp. 217–18, still one of the best critical essays on *Ulysses*.

60. *U.*, pp. 686 ff. (855 ff.; 710 ff.).

61. Cp. the attacks in Wyndham Lewis, *Time and Western Man*, London 1927, BK I, ch. 16; and D. S. Savage, *The Withered Branch*, London 1950, pp. 156 ff.

62. E., p. 551.

63. *Dublin's Joyce*, ch. 14.

64. Cp. A. G. Lehmann, *The Symbolist Aesthetic in France, 1885–1895*, Oxford 1950, pp. 242 ff.

65. Cp. P. Toynbee, "A Study of James Joyce's *Ulysses*," in *T.D.C.*, pp. 272 ff.

66. *L.*, p. 180; cp. p. 170. For other interesting statements of intention, see pp. 135, 139, 146–7, 152, 160.

67. *E.g.* Kenner, *Dublin's Joyce*, p. 262.

CHAPTER V

HOW MUCH LAND DOES A MAN NEED?

Let me say at the outset that I do not believe *Finnegans Wake* is worth detailed exegesis. There are many who think otherwise, of course, and they have explained a good deal about the book: its "literal" situation (the Dublin publican, H. C. Earwicker, his family, his dream); its mythology (the archetypal lover-husband-father H.C.E., the mistress-wife-mother A.L.P., the twins Shem and Shaun, the lover-daughter; the Viconian cycles of history; the polarities of Bruno's identical opposites; the eternal themes of love, marriage, crime, judgment, war, civilisation and decay, fall and resurrection, etc.); its technical devices (the merging of heroes and situations, the circular structure, the recurrent *"motifs,"* the allusions, parodies, esoteric "symbolism," the pervasive verbal play, etc.).[1] There is even an indispensable (if not always convincing) *Skeleton Key* to this gigantic, erudite, amalgamated "monomyth" of human life. Undoubtedly it will always be a happy hunting-ground for what passes as "scholarship" and "research," and some of the results may even prove relevant enough to help explain what Joyce was about. Nevertheless, the work itself seems to me an artistic failure; and despite the enthusiastic assertions of its admirers, the questions it prompts the ordinary reader to ask remain, I believe, still the most important—questions concerned less with its verbal "meaning" or its machinery than with its value: why Joyce ever undertook it, why it seems so laborious and, more particularly, so unrewarding to read through.

One thing we must grant is the seriousness of its in-

tention. It arose not from mere *avant-garde* intoxication
but from one of the central problems of our age: to
discover what a fully unified, fully human vitality might
be. Ever since the Romantics, art has endeavoured (in
Shelley's apposite phrase) to compel us "to feel that
which we perceive, and to imagine that which we know."
Terms like "life," "organic," "vitality," have played a
key role in all our thinking. The artist and thinker alike
have sought to "see into the life of things," to apprehend
a Reality in which the "dissociations" of our world—
between nature and man, for example, or fact and value,
or thinking and feeling, or necessity and freedom—will
be healed, and in which both the individual and society
can find the sustaining source and pattern of their life.
At first the Romantic artist saw his own search as a
symbol of the problem; then, as Romanticism became
conscious of itself in Symbolism (if so crude a formula
may serve), he began to see his own search as a symbol
of the answer.

Joyce's career offers almost a model of this whole
process. From his early Romantic egoism he came
eventually to discover the meaning of "life," first in the
creative understanding wherein he defined himself *as* a
creative artist, and then in the more complex act wherein
he defined the social and moral nature of his world and
of himself. The critical exploration of the self led, with
an exemplary logic, to the critical exploration of society.
By the end of *Ulysses*, however, he came to a further
problem. It was clear that the only forms of moral,
social, and artistic life available in the modern world
could not contain, or even sanction, the whole potential
life of a Bloom, much less that of his creator. If, as the
Portrait and *Ulysses* subtly insist, the individual realises
himself only as he discovers his life-values in the shape
and meaning he finds-and-creates in his experience, the
end result is a radical scepticism about any society, any
institution, and indeed any artistic creation. The search

for "life" must now proceed beyond all these—to what the individual (artist or citizen) and the particular "now and here" (Dublin–1904 or Paris–1922) share with all men and all societies, what the individual work of art shares with every human "Word." In what reality does *mankind* find the source and pattern of its life? The answer could only be the meaning of human history itself. And so Joyce was led to the aspiration announced at the beginning of the nineteenth century and lurking ever since beneath the relativism of our age, beneath its historicism, its concern with psychology, anthropology, myth, symbolic form, language itself. He would confront Life directly, beyond the provisional forms of fiction, and write a comprehensive epic of Humanity, a "monomyth" of all the myths, the "Words," by which Man has ordered his experience and therein "understood" reality and realised himself *as* Man.

Such a work would take both Joyce's career and his art to their logical conclusion. Vico's *New Science* was perhaps the first history of Man's self-realisation through the "Words" he found for his experience; and just as Vico had seen that his own philosophic "Word" was the necessary culmination of the process it expounded, so could Joyce see his monomyth. For Vico the successive stages of the human spirit—the Religious, the Heroic, and the Civil—reached intellectual self-understanding in his own history of them, and must therefore once again begin their unfolding on a higher plane of consciousness; for Joyce, his "monomyth" would analogously express the crisis of modern civilisation and also reach the ultimate goal of Symbolistic art. Being both a comprehensive portrayal and a comprehensive example of the creative understanding of Man, it would become one with the reality it represented. It would be both a reflexion and a part of its own subject—as the *Portrait* had been—but now expressing a "universal" self-understanding, the author discovering in his experience of the world the

H

pattern not only of the Romantic artist or the modern citizen, but of *homo sapiens*. It would (if we may describe one aspect of the form of *Finnegans Wake* in the manner of another) achieve the Symbolist bliss of being swallowed by its own tale.

There is no mystery, therefore, about the "argument" of *Finnegans Wake*. Indeed, it tells us, quite clearly, again and again: It portrays the course of history, which seems at first sight only a meaningless "collideorscape,"[2] a chaotic, "undivided reawlity"[3] or a "one-horse" performance by "Messrs. Thud and Blunder. . . . Promptings by Elanio Vitale."[4] Nevertheless, we can apprehend recurrent patterns in the flux, "the same tale" told differently of all men, all societies, all civilisations.[5] For all of us come into our world like little pigs "in a poke"; we express our sense of our destiny in religious beliefs (as children do in make-believe games); marriages have to be made, property established, work performed; we obey, and we create, the never very satisfactory institutions of our world; life declines and yet renews itself; through the perpetual "wake" of life we enjoy what we can of "these secret workings of natures."[6] The same pattern is repeated in each stage through which the human spirit has grown; "the Vico road goes round and round to meet where terms begin"[7]—its shape is the necessary shape of life itself. And life speaks itself, is realised or (to use Joyce's old term) "epiphanised," in all the "scriptsigns,"[8] the "nameforms,"[9] the institutions, the deeds, in which man has expressed both "objective" reality and his own "subjective" being. Any one epiphany reflects the whole "macromass,"[10] for it is not merely representative of, but a necessary step in, the process of life's self-comprehension. Perhaps the clearest and greatest of such epiphanies is the creation (or discovery) of the symbolic instrument of the alphabet—"allforabit";[11] it enables life to realise itself further in the development of language, in the highly self-conscious traditions of literature, and even, we must add, in the mass degeneration of language in our own decaying Civil Age.[12]

In apprehending the substance of Life, personal identity appears merely accidental.[13] The hero is any man, for all men contain and reflect the male experience—as we see it, for example, even in the topographical relationship of hill to river. The hero is Finnegan, or H. C. Everybody,[14] "human, erring and condonable,"[15] or Swift, or the author himself, whose "egourge" contains all the essential "celves" of human experience.[16] The combination of "truth and untruth"[17] enables man to imagine ("Sham") the possibilities he contains and so to possess himself more fully through his creative activity. By shamming, by being "not a man," he answers the first and last "riddle of the universe":[18] what is man? He discovers himself, as Bloom and Stephen did, in traversing the "Heroes' Highway where our fleshers leave their bonings."[19] To ask why life takes the patterns it does, unfolds in the process it does, can only be answered in one way: "Such me."[20] Such (search) Everybody.

Thus the "autobiographical" Shem-the-Penman chapter,[21] like all the others, reflects the universal pattern from its particular position within it. It focuses on the implications of the creative act, the *felix culpa* in which man both disrupts an existing order and fulfils the order of his becoming: on the necessary self-division of the "celves," the doubt, the obloquy; the unfolding of the familial and other possibilities of man; the expense of energy that simultaneously carries him a step towards both life and death.[22] Like all mankind's creative activity, *Finnegans Wake* is a "letter selfpenned to one's other... neverperfect everplanned.... [a] nonday diary ... allnights newseryreel."[23] As a work of art, however, it claims to represent that activity in its purest form: in our everyday space-world, only the Gracehoper's song can "beat time."[24] Shem, the artist who can make the

dead awaken and speak,[25] is "the shining keyman of the
wilds of change";[26] and we can see why the book ends
with: "The keys to. Given! A way a lone a last a loved a
long the"[27] specifying no conclusion except the necessary
repetition of the same enterprise, and none of the in-
numerable worlds in which it has been or may be
performed.

Finnegans Wake is thus a "Book of Lief"[28]—written by
Joyce ("authordux") in one sense, but in another written
by the language of everybody. In describing the mys-
terious "letter," which would explain everything in the
dream if it could only be deciphered, it really describes
itself. As the letter is to *Finnegans Wake* so is the book to
the manifold of human experience. The letter was written by life, and misdelivered and defaced by life; perhaps
all we can read of it is Alpha and Omega, with an
exclamation and a question-mark between.[29] It is an
"epistola of their weatherings and their marryings and
their buryings and their natural selections" told in any
and every language.[30] Its interpretation is all in the eye of
the beholder, for it is composed of the whole flux of
human "scriptsigns,"[31] a moving puzzle reminding us
"ineluctably of nature at her naturalest."[32] And hence
the peculiar "idioglossary"[33] in which *Finnegans Wake* is
written. It is a language composed of, and reflecting, as
many "scriptsigns" as possible[34]—a language to represent
(in both senses of that word) its own significance *as*
language. It finds its artistic programme in exploiting
its own symbolic status.

This, briefly, is the structure of Joyce's intentions, the
reality he tries to "render" to us and to shape as he does
so. The result, however, is so dubious that it raises
doubts about the whole logic out of which the work arose.

Probably every reader can enjoy some bits of it.
Occasionally it does achieve the weird fluidity of a
dream.[35] Many passages are extremely funny (as Joyce
could often be), and particularly so when the writing

exploits a racy or absurd vernacular.[36] Sometimes there is real (if fragmentary) wit or satire in the word-play.[37] There are flashes of Joyce's crisp and delightful vivacity;[38] many passages of a self-conscious, but complex and unstrained lyricism.[39] One cannot but be moved by the ending—Anna Liffey's song as she flows homewards and yet deathwards to the sea, where the irresistible momentum plays against nostalgia for the past, celebration against bitter lament. Here one feels the author and his work *are* impersonally one. But however much the reader may admire passages, this does not, as one critic remarks,[40] amount to admiring the book. Nor does it dispose of the vast amount (*e.g.* most of Books 2 and 3) that is simply boring—boring not so much because it is "obscure" as because it obviously has so little to say that we do not care whether it is "obscure" or not.

The central trouble with the work, however, derives from the very nature of its intention, from the universe it presents for us to imagine. That universe could briefly be described in the terms of another Symbolistic writer, Emerson: man is no more than "the faculty of reporting," the world no more than "the possibility of being reported." Joyce himself said that the debate between Bishop Berkeley and St Patrick[41] expressed the defence and the indictment of his book;[42] and the central issue there is precisely that of Emerson's doctrine: the identity of the artistic symbol (*i.e.* the work) with the world it constitutes and with the person through whom it is realised, so that the artist, his act of "meaning," and the meaning of things are finally indistinguishable. In the act of expressing his symbol, man himself becomes a symbol of a wholly organic, wholly symbolic universe. "There is no fact in nature," said Emerson, "which does not carry the whole sense of nature"; "the entire system of things gets represented in every particle"; in an ideal language, every word would be "million-faced."[43] Life is an infinite potentiality of meaning.

The objections to beliefs like Emerson's also apply to *Finnegans Wake*, and Joyce obviously recognised some of them himself. He knew he had to balance "the consequences and the necessity of his method,"[44] to try to make a finite work express the in-finiteness of Life, and even to accept the possible uselessness of his work to others. He saw that the reader, faced with its rambling texture,[45] its "imperfectible moral blindness," its "too-muchness" and "fartoomanyness,"[46] its "meticulosity bordering on the insane,"[47] might well exclaim, "why, O why, O why?"[48] In spite of all this (and of the objections to *Work in Progress*) he was convinced that his reasons were sufficient; and by adopting the criticisms as his own and writing them into the work itself he fell back on the old tactic of defensive self-mockery. What he could not afford to recognise was the self-defeating nature of his ambition. For if he succeeded in expressing *all* that could be expressed, if he included *all* the potentialities of Life, if his work did become one with himself and with Reality, his art would supersede itself. This, of course, has been the haunting "death wish" of art at least since the Romantics—the desire (which has taken many forms) not merely "to see into the life of things" but to *become* the life of things. Joyce's own insistence on "the classical temper," his tortuously evolved aesthetic, his mature conception of "drama," exemplify the forces that held this desire in check, though its pressure can be detected in all his works. In the end, however, it seems to have escaped, or rather to have converted his very defences to its own use. The more comprehensively he tried to see "life," the less potent his work became as art; the "drama of the whole" turned into the death of "drama."

All the objections to *Finnegans Wake*—both those Joyce recognised and those he did not—arise, I think, from this absence of "drama."[49] In the universe of the *Wake*, elements like precise observation and characterisation, consistent conventions, narrative structure, economy or inevitability of style, are necessarily insignificant. The various "selves" (or "characters" or "voices") are only "cells" of one gigantic whole; they do not enact drama, but exemplify laws, necessities beyond purpose, responsibility, victory, or defeat. There can be no discrimination between the actual and the possible; things, as we know them in everyday life, are only one symbolic fiction among others. It is impossible to call any of the word-play pointless. In the absence of "drama," of any real "now and here," there is no way of denying the relevance, or even the existence, of any meaning any commentator cares to find in the words. Language is infinitely exploited and exploitable, for nothing creates any limit to its capacity to mean.

When Joyce asks, "It was life but was it fair? It was free but was it art?"[50] we can respond only from our own sense of what life is; and whether *Finnegans Wake* is free or fair, whatever its value as autobiography or verbal experimentation or anything else, it is for me neither life nor art. Indeed, I would invoke the support both of *Ulysses* and of the insight on which its achievement rests: that we understand life (or imagine truly) only as individuals, necessarily living in and by means of our particular circumstances. Our physical limitations (being "ineluctable") may be seen as the grounds of comedy or tragedy or, as in the *Portrait* and *Ulysses*, a complex kind of irony involving both. Nevertheless, without those limits we could not apprehend any true meaning in our experience because we could not engage the whole of our being in the act of apprehension. To imagine *truly*, to understand *reality*, involves us in choices. We have to decide about the presence, and nature, and relative status, of any "meaning" we confront. Our values, like those of Bloom or Stephen, are what we make of the world. And truly to imagine, really to understand, the whole History of Man or the Nature of Life can only be a theoretical possibility, a quite notional experience. To apprehend *everything* is to express mere potentiality as such—an enterprise in which the idea of error or distortion must lose its meaning, and with it, too, the possibility of choice and value. In the quasi-divine contemplation of *Finnegans Wake*, therefore, language and form can only freewheel in a boundless empyrean. With *Ulysses* it is not absurd to use the same terms as we might apply to *The Divine Comedy*: that it holds to, even as it transcends, all the specific choices, the enacted values, in which we discover our selves, or "life," or art. That transcending is its "drama." *Finnegans Wake*, on the other hand, merely assumes its "vision" and so it merely supersedes choice and value from the start.

The result is the most fundamental weakness of all: the book can only tell us its "argument"; it cannot realise it imaginatively. The language—despite its air of tremendous activity, despite the odd occasions when it does manage to relate disparate experiences—is generally *inert*. The following is a representative example (H.C.E. is about to tell a story in his pub):

> ... And then. Be old. The next thing is. We are once amore as babes awondering in a wold made fresh where with the hen in the storyaboot we start from scratch.
>
> So the truce, the old truce and nattonbuff the truce, boys. Drouth is stronger than faction. Slant. Shinshin. Shinshin.[51]

In its way, this is quite funny. As for its more serious intentions, there is a reason, no doubt, for "amore" (*e.g.* the Tristram "theme"), or "the wold made fresh" (the world made flesh), or "truce," or "nattonbuff" (*e.g.* the "theme" of Buckley and the Russian general); and so on. We might wonder about "storyaboot" or "shinshin"; but then, indeed, what is *any* of these particular spellings doing? Can the various "themes" and meanings be said to be *imaginatively* fused in them?—or even imaginatively *present*?[52] Like most of the book, in fact, the language here seems to me to heighten the very dissociations it tries to bridge. For the reader, as for Macbeth, "function | Is smother'd in surmise; and nothing is | But what is not"; and the effect is to encourage him to analyse, *i.e.* to separate, the fixities and definites collected by Joyce's Fancy.

Finnegans Wake is obviously the response of a "cunning artist" to "the breakdown of public standards of value and significance."[53] But the word "response" is ambiguous. To suppose (as Joyce and his admirers were occasionally wont to do) that it is a nonce-work, so to speak, a unique experiment that need not affect the language or art of anyone else,[54] is to evade the question of why art matters at all. *Finnegans Wake* is not merely a personal reaction to an abstract situation, one which we ought to accept on a blind faith in Literature (or in Joyce as a Great Writer). It is a particular instance of that situation, a situation of which we ourselves are part, and we cannot avoid judging it and pondering the implications of our judgment. Perhaps Joyce always loved people and things too little. Certainly his imagination seems to have withered among rootless abstractions: most of the over-elaborate "schema" was added to *Ulysses* after 1920,[55] the year in which he also moved to Paris, and *Finnegans Wake* almost confesses his own sense of tiredness, withdrawal, approaching exhaustion. But perhaps it also reveals a weakness in modern thinking—a tendency to take the medium of life for the substance, to expect too much of art or language or even of consciousness itself. In our desire to know more and more of life, and to possess even ourselves in complete and perfect selfconsciousness, we tend to forget (as Joyce perhaps forgot) that we can never see behind our own heads, and that, as we have finally to choose what we are, so we have finally to choose what we really know among all possible "truths" and "meanings." Similarly, we can dream of mastering the whole of life (as Joyce perhaps dreamed of doing) by surrendering to language or art, only if we forget the values necessarily engaged in them. *Finnegans Wake* fails to heal the dissociations of our experience in an all-embracing vision of Life; but what possibly could do so?

Joyce's career offers us the image of a dilemma far wider than his own. From Stephen to Bloom to Molly to *Finnegans Wake*; and at the end he is said to have been contemplating a book about the Sea,[56] the Ultimate towards which *Finnegans Wake* flows: perhaps an even more abstract work, to which someone like Darwin or Teilhard de Chardin might have been the Vico? On the other hand, there is his remark in a letter to his daughter: "In my opinion *How Much Land Does a Man Need* is the greatest story that the literature of the world knows."[57] He would not have been Joyce if he had failed to see the bearing on his own case either of Tolstoy's story or of his judgment of it, and we might allow it to stand as the final comment not only on his lifelong theme, but on both the achievement and the limitations of his work.

REFERENCES

1. The best introductory account is probably still Levin, *James Joyce*, pp. 121 ff.
2. *F.W.*, p. 143.
3. *Op. cit.*, p. 292.
4. *Op. cit.*, p. 221.
5. *Op. cit.*, pp. 18, 481.
6. *Op. cit.*, pp. 613 ff.
7. *Op. cit.*, p. 452.
8. *Op. cit.*, p. 118.
9. *Op. cit.*, p. 18.
10. *Op. cit.*, p. 111.
11. *Op. cit.*, p. 19.
12. *Op. cit.*, pp. 18–20.
13. *Op. cit.*, pp. 49, 51.
14. *Op. cit.*, p. 32.
15. *Op. cit.*, p. 58.
16. *Op. cit.*, pp. 49–50.
17. *Op. cit.*, p. 169.
18. *Op. cit.*, pp. 170, 607.
19. *Op. cit.*, p. 607.
20. *Op. cit.*, p. 597.
21. *Op. cit.*, pp. 169 ff.
22. *Op. cit.*, pp. 184 ff.
23. *Op. cit.*, p. 489.
24. *Op. cit.*, pp. 415, 419.
25. *Op. cit.*, p. 195.
26. *Op. cit.*, p. 186.
27. *Op. cit.*, p. 628.

28. *Op. cit.*, p. 425.

29. *Op. cit.*, pp. 93–4, 420 ff.

30. *Op. cit.*, p. 117.

31. *Op. cit.*, p. 118.

32. *Op. cit.*, p. 120.

33. *Op. cit.*, p. 423.

34. *Op. cit.*, pp. 18–20, 111, etc.

35. *E.g. op. cit.*, pp. 196 ff.

36. *Op. cit.*, pp. 8 ff., 39–40, 462 ff.

37. *Op. cit.*, pp. 64–5, 142–3, 431 ff., 573 ff.

38. *Op. cit.*, pp. 226–7, 414 ff.

39. *Op. cit.*, pp. 215–16, 258–9, 556.

40. Daiches, *The Novel and the Modern World*, pp. 135–6.

41. *F.W.*, pp. 611–12.

42. *L.*, p. 406. For a reading of the "debate," see Campbell and Robinson, *A Skeleton Key to Finnegans Wake*, London 1947, p. 286. Cp. A. Walton Litz, *The Art of James Joyce*, London 1961, pp. 78–9; J. S. Atherton, *The Books at the Wake*, London 1959, pp. 97–9.

43. See C. Feidelson Jr, *Symbolism and American Literature*, Chicago 1953, pp. 144–9.

44. *Op. cit.*, ch. 2, esp. pp. 71–4.

45. *F.W.*, pp. 41–2, 246–7.

46. *Op. cit.*, p. 122.

47. *Op. cit.*, p. 173. For Joyce's methods of composition, see Litz, *Art of James Joyce*, ch. 3.

48. *F.W.*, p. 123.

49. *E.g.* Edmund Wilson, "The Dream of H. C. Ear-wicker," in *T.D.C.*, pp. 319 ff., and Levin, *James Joyce*, pp. 150 ff. More searching criticisms are F. R. Leavis, "James Joyce and 'The Revolution of the Word'," in *Scrutiny*, II (1933), pp. 193 ff.; Savage, *The Withered Branch*, pp. 191 ff.; J. Peter, "Joyce and the Novel," in *Kenyon Review*, XVIII (1956), pp. 619 ff.; D. Donoghue, "Joyce and the Finite Order," in *Sewanee Review*, LXVIII (1960), pp. 256 ff.

50. *F.W.*, p. 94.

51. *Op. cit.*, p. 336.

52. Cp. Litz., *Art of James Joyce*, pp. 60–2, 79, 96–8, for an intelligent exegete's embarrassment in using *active* verbs like "suggest," "imply," "express," etc. about the language of *Finnegans Wake*.

53. Cp. Daiches, *The Novel and the Modern World*, p. 134.

54. E., p. 559; and S. Gilbert, "Prolegomena to *Work in Progress*," in Samuel Beckett *et al.*, *Our Exagmination*, London 1936, p. 57.

55. Litz, *Art of James Joyce*, pp. 29 ff.

56. L. Gillet, *Claybook for James Joyce*, trans. G. Markow-Totevy, London and New York 1958, p. 119.

57. *L.*, p. 364.

BIBLIOGRAPHY

I. MAIN WORKS OF JAMES JOYCE

I have drawn most of the following information from John J. Slocum and Herbert Cahoon: *A Bibliography of James Joyce*, London 1953, which should be consulted for further details. In this section of the bibliography I have listed the place, publisher, and date of the first English and the first American editions of Joyce's works. In general, references in the text are to currently available editions; these are marked with an asterisk.

1. Early Essays, and Poetry

"Ibsen's New Drama," in *Fortnightly Review*, LXVII (1900), pp. 575 ff.

"The Day of the Rabblement," in F. J. C. Skeffington and James A. Joyce, *Two Essays*, Dublin 1901.

"James Clarence Mangan," in *St. Stephen's* (Dublin), 1, No. 6 (1902), pp. 116 ff.

The Holy Office, Pola 1904.

All the above are included, with various other minor writings, in
* *The Critical Writings of James Joyce*, ed. Ellsworth Mason and Richard Ellmann.

Chamber Music, London (Elkin Mathews) 1907; New York (Huebsch) 1918, * (Columbia) 1954, ed. William York Tindall.

Pomes Penyeach, Paris 1927; New York (Sylvia Beach) 1931; London (Harmsworth) 1932, (Faber) 1933.

Collected Poems, New York (Black Sun) 1936, (Viking) 1937.

The contents of the three above are included in *The Essential James Joyce*, ed. Harry Levin.

2. Fiction

Dubliners, London (Grant Richards) 1914, * (Cape) 1954; New York (Huebsch) 1916, * (Modern Library) 1926.

A Portrait of the Artist as a Young Man (First appeared serially in *The Egoist* (London) 1914–15). New York (Huebsch) 1916, * (Modern Library) 1928; London (Egoist) 1917, * (Cape) 1956.

Ulysses (Parts first appeared serially in *The Little Review* (New York) 1918–20 and *The Egoist* (London) 1919). Paris 1922; London (Egoist) 1922, * (Bodley Head) 1937, * (Bodley Head) 1960; New York (Random House) 1934, * (Modern Library) 1940.

Finnegans Wake (Fragments were first published serially in *transition* (Paris) 1927–38, and in book form as: *Anna Livia Plurabelle*, New York (Gaige) 1928, London (Faber) 1930; *Tales Told of Shem and Shaun*, Paris 1929, London (Faber) 1932 (slightly different form); *Haveth Childers Everywhere*, Paris-New York (Fountain Press) 1930, London (Faber) 1931; *The Mime of Mick Nick and*

the Maggies, The Hague–Paris–London (Faber)–New York
(Gotham Book Mart) 1934; *Storiella as She is Syung*, London
(Corvinus) 1937.) London (Faber) 1939; New York (Viking)
1939 (pagination the same).

Stephen Hero, ed. Theodore Spencer, London (Cape) 1944; New York
(New Directions) 1944. Revised edition, with additional material
ed. John J. Slocum and Herbert Cahoon, * New York (New
Directions) 1955; * London (Cape) 1956.

Epiphanies, ed. O. A. Silverman, Lockwood Memorial Library,
University of Buffalo, 1956.

3. Drama

Exiles, London (Grant Richards) 1918, * 1952 (Cape), edited, with
the author's notes, by Padraic Colum; New York (Huebsch)
1918, ed. Colum (Viking) 1951.

4. Collections and Miscellaneous

The Portable James Joyce, ed. Harry Levin, New York (Viking) 1947;
also published as * *The Essential James Joyce*, London (Cape)
1948 (Includes *Dubliners*, *A Portrait of the Artist*, *Exiles*, *Collected
Poems*, *The Holy Office*, *Gas From a Burner*, and selections from
Ulysses and *Finnegans Wake*).

Letters of James Joyce, ed. Stuart Gilbert, * London (Faber) 1957;
New York (Viking) 1957 (Additional letters, etc., are also published in Richard Ellmann, *James Joyce*).

"A Portrait of the Artist" (1904), in Richard M. Kain and Robert E.
Scholes, "The First Version of Joyce's 'Portrait'," in *The Yale
Review*, LXIX (1960), pp. 355 ff.

The Critical Writings of James Joyce, ed. by Ellsworth Mason and
Richard Ellmann, * London (Faber) 1959; New York (Viking)
1959 (Includes among other material: "Drama and Life,"
"Ibsen's New Drama," "The Day of the Rabblement," "James
Clarence Mangan," book reviews (1902–3), the Paris and Pola
notebooks (1903–4), *The Holy Office*, political articles (1907–12),
Gas From a Burner, etc.).

II. OTHERS

For fuller lists see M. Magalaner and R. M. Kain, *Joyce*, pp. 351 ff.,
and Maurice Beebe and Walton Litz, "Criticism of James Joyce:
A Selected Checklist," in *Modern Fiction Studies*, IV (1958), pp.
71 ff.; and Robert H. Deming, *A Bibliography of James Joyce
Studies*, University of Kansas Libraries, 1964.

ADAMS, ROBERT M.: *Surface and Symbol, The Consistency of James Joyce's
Ulysses*, N.Y. 1962.

ATHERTON, JAMES S.: *The Books at the Wake*, London 1959.

BAKER, JAMES R.: "Joyce's *Chamber Music*: The Exile of the Heart," in *Arizona Quarterly*, XV (1959), pp. 349 ff.

BEEBE, MAURICE and LITZ, WALTON: "Criticism of James Joyce: A Selected Checklist," in *Modern Fiction Studies*, IV (1958), pp. 71 ff.

BEEBE, MAURICE: "Joyce and Stephen Dedalus: The Problem of Autobiography," in *A James Joyce Miscellany, Second Series*, ed. Marvin Magalaner, Carbondale, Ill. 1959, pp. 67 ff.

BLACKMUR, R. P.: "The Jew in Search of a Son," *Virginia Quarterly Review*, XXIV (1948), pp. 96 ff.

BUDGEN, FRANK: *James Joyce and the Making of Ulysses*, London 1934; * London 1937.

CAMPBELL, JOSEPH and ROBINSON, HENRY MORTON: *A Skeleton Key to Finnegans Wake*, New York 1944; * London 1947.

CONNOLLY, THOMAS E.: "Stephen Hero Revisited," in *The James Joyce Review*, III (1959), pp. 40 ff.

——— (ed.): *Joyce's Portrait, Criticism and Critiques*, New York 1962, London 1964.

COPE, JACKSON I.: "The Rhythmic Gesture: Image and Aesthetic in Joyce's *Ulysses*," in *E.L.H.* XXIX (1962), pp. 67 ff.

DAICHES, DAVID: *The Novel and the Modern World*, Chicago 1939; * revised edn. Chicago and Cambridge 1960.

DONOGHUE, DENIS: "Joyce and the Finite Order," in *Sewanee Review*, LXVIII (1960), pp. 256 ff.

ELLMANN, RICHARD: "Ulysses the Divine Nobody," in *Yale Review*, XLVII (1957), pp. 56 ff.

———: *James Joyce*, New York 1959.

FARRELL, JAMES T.: *The League of Frightened Philistines and Other Papers*, London 1948.

———: "Exiles and Ibsen," in *James Joyce: Two Decades of Criticism*, ed. Seon Givens, New York 1948, pp. 95 ff.

FEIDELSON, CHARLES, JR: *Symbolism and American Literature*, Chicago 1953.

FERGUSSON, FRANCIS: *The Human Image in Dramatic Literature*, New York 1957.

FRIEDMAN, MELVIN: *Stream of Consciousness: A Study in Literary Method*, New Haven 1955.

GHISELIN, BREWSTER: "The Unity of James Joyce's *Dubliners*," in *Accent*, XVI (1956), pp. 75 ff, 196 ff.

GILBERT, STUART: "Prolegomena to *Work in Progress*," in Samuel Beckett and others, *Our Exagmination Round His Factification For Incamination of Work in Progress*, Paris 1929; * enlarged edn. London 1936, pp. 47 ff.

———: *James Joyce's Ulysses*, London 1930; * revised edn. London 1952.

GILLET, LOUIS: *Claybook for James Joyce*, Paris 1946; * trans. Georges Markow-Totevy, London and New York, 1958.

GIVENS, SEON (ed.): *James Joyce: Two Decades of Criticism*, New York 1948.

GLASHEEN, ADELINE: *A Second Census of Finnegans Wake*, Northwestern University 1963.

GOLDBERG, S. L.: *The Classical Temper*, London and New York 1961.

GOLDMAN, ARNOLD: *The Joyce Paradox*, London 1966.

HART, CLIVE: *Structure and Motif in Finnegans Wake*, London 1962.

HUMPHREY, ROBERT: *Stream of Consciousness in the Modern Novel*, Berkeley and Los Angeles 1954.

JACK, JANE H.: "Art and *The Portrait of the Artist*," in *Essays in Criticism*, V (1955), pp. 354 ff. and in *Joyce's Portrait, Criticisms and Critiques*, ed. Thomas Connolly, New York 1962, London 1964.

JOLAS, MARIA: "Joyce's Friend Jolas," in *A James Joyce Miscellany*, ed. Marvin Magalaner, New York (James Joyce Society) 1957, pp. 62 ff.

JOYCE, STANISLAUS: *My Brother's Keeper*, London 1958.

KAIN, RICHARD M.: *Fabulous Voyager*, Chicago 1947.

—— and SCHOLES, ROBERT E.: "The First Version of Joyce's 'Portrait'," in *Yale Review*, LXIX (1960), pp. 355 ff.

KENNER, HUGH: *Dublin's Joyce*, London 1955.

KNIGHT, DOUGLAS: "The Reading of *Ulysses*," in *ELH*, XIX (1952), pp. 64 ff.

LEAVIS, F. R.: "James Joyce and 'The Revolution of the Word'," in *Scrutiny*, II (1933), pp. 193 ff.

LEHMANN, A. G.: *The Symbolist Aesthetic in France, 1885–1895*, Oxford 1950.

LEVIN, HARRY: *James Joyce, A Critical Introduction*, Norfolk, Conn. 1941; * revised edn. London 1960.

—— (ed.): *The Essential James Joyce*, New York 1947; * London 1948.

LEWIS, WYNDHAM: *Time and Western Man*, London 1927.

LITZ, A. WALTON: *The Art of James Joyce*, London 1961.

MACLEOD, VIVIENNE KOCH: "The Influence of Ibsen on Joyce," in *Publications of the Modern Language Association of America*, LX (1945), pp. 877 ff.

MAGALANER, MARVIN (ed.): *A James Joyce Miscellany*, New York (James Joyce Society) 1957.

—— (ed.): *A James Joyce Miscellany, Second Series*, Carbondale, Ill. 1959.

——: *Time of Apprenticeship: The Fiction of the Young James Joyce*, New York and London 1959.

—— and KAIN, RICHARD M.: *Joyce: the Man, the Work, the Reputation*, New York 1956.

MASON, ELLSWORTH: "James Joyce, Moralist," in *Twentieth Century Literature*, I (1956), pp. 196 ff.

OSTROFF, ANTHONY: "The Moral Vision in 'Dubliners'," in *Western Speech*, XX (1956), pp. 196 ff.

PETER, JOHN: "Joyce and the Novel," in *Kenyon Review*, XVIII (1956), pp. 619 ff.

POSS, S. H.: "A Portrait of the Artist as Beginner," in *University of Kansas City Review*, XXVI (1960), pp. 189 ff.

POUND, EZRA: "Ulysses" (1922), in his *Literary Essays*, London 1954.

PRESCOTT, JOSEPH: *Exploring James Joyce*, Carbondale 1964.

SAVAGE, D. S.: *The Withered Branch*, London 1950.

SCHORER, MARK: "Technique as Discovery," in *Forms of Modern Fiction*, ed. W. Van O'Connor, Minneapolis 1948, pp. 9 ff.

SLOCUM, JOHN J. and CAHOON, HERBERT: *A Bibliography of James Joyce*, London 1953.

TATE, ALLEN: "Three Commentaries," in *Sewanee Review*, LVIII (1950), pp. 1 ff.

TINDALL, WILLIAM YORK: *James Joyce, His Way of Interpreting the Modern World*, New York and London 1950.

——: *A Reader's Guide to James Joyce*, New York 1959.

TOYNBEE, PHILIP: "A Study of James Joyce's Ulysses," in *James Joyce: Two Decades of Criticism*, ed. Seon Givens, New York 1948, pp. 243 ff.

VAN GHENT, DOROTHY: *The English Novel, Form and Function*, New York 1953.

WILLIAMS, RAYMOND: "The 'Exiles' of James Joyce," in *Politics and Letters*, 1 (1948), pp. 13 ff.

WILSON, EDMUND: *Axel's Castle*, New York 1931; *New York and London 1950.

——: "The Dream of H. C. Earwicker," in his *The Wound and the Bow*, New York 1947, and *in *James Joyce: Two Decades of Criticism*, ed. Seon Givens, New York 1948, pp. 319 ff.

WOODWARD, A. G.: "Technique and Feeling in James Joyce's *A Portrait of the Artist as a Young Man*," in *English Studies in Africa*, IV (1961), pp. 39 ff.